W9-BAP-387

Genetics

Genetics

Other books in The Lucent Library of Science and Technology include:

Black Holes
Comets and Asteroids
Global Warming
Lasers

The Lucent Library of SCIENCE AND TECHNOLOGY

Genetics

by Robert Taylor

LUCENT
BOOKS®

THOMSON
★
GALE

San Diego • Detroit • New York • San Francisco • Cleveland • New Haven, Conn. • Waterville, Maine • London • Munich

On cover: Twin boys relax in the sunshine. The study of genetics helps us understand why twins look alike.

LIBRARY OF CONGRESS CATALOGING-IN-PUBLICATION DATA

Taylor, Robert, 1948–
  Genetics / by Robert Taylor
    p. cm. — (The Lucent library of science and technology)
  Summary: Discusses the history and current state of scientific understanding of genetics, exploring the roles of genes, DNA, and RNA, as well as the medical, legal, and ethical dimensions of such issues as genetic engineering and DNA evidence.
  Includes bibliographical references and index.
    ISBN 1-59018-103-4 (lib. bdg. : alk. paper)
    1. Genetics—Juvenile literature. [1. Genetics.] I. Title. II. Series.
  QH437.5.T39 2004
  576.5—dc22

                                                                    2003014088

Printed in the United States of America

Table of Contents

Foreword

"The world has changed far more in the past 100 years than in any other century in history. The reason is not political or economic, but technological—technologies that flowed directly from advances in basic science."

— Stephen Hawking, "A Brief History of Relativity," *Time,* 2000

The twentieth-century scientific and technological revolution that British physicist Stephen Hawking describes in the above quote has transformed virtually every aspect of human life at an unprecedented pace. Inventions unimaginable a century ago have not only become commonplace but are now considered necessities of daily life. As science historian James Burke writes, "We live surrounded by objects and systems that we take for granted, but which profoundly affect the way we behave, think, work, play, and in general conduct our lives."

For example, in just one hundred years, transportation systems have dramatically changed. In 1900 the first gasoline-powered motorcar had just been introduced, and only 144 miles of U.S. roads were hard-surfaced. Horse-drawn trolleys still filled the streets of American cities. The airplane had yet to be invented. Today 217 million vehicles speed along 4 million miles of U.S. roads. Humans have flown to the moon and commercial aircraft are capable of transporting passengers across the Atlantic Ocean in less than three hours.

The transformation of communications has been just as dramatic. In 1900 most Americans lived and worked on farms without electricity or mail delivery. Few people had ever heard a radio or spoken on a telephone. A hundred years later, 98 percent of American homes have telephones and televisions and more than 50 percent have personal computers. Some families even have more than one television and computer, and cell phones are now commonplace, even among the young. Data beamed from communication satellites routinely predict global weather conditions and fiber-optic cable, e-mail, and the Internet have made worldwide telecommunication instantaneous.

Perhaps the most striking measure of scientific and technological change can be seen in medicine and public health. At the beginning of the twentieth century, the average American life span was forty-seven years. By the end of the century the average life span was approaching eighty years, thanks to advances in medicine including the development of vaccines and antibiotics, the discovery of powerful diagnostic tools such as X rays, the life-saving technology of cardiac and neonatal care, and improvements in nutrition and the control of infectious disease.

Rapid change is likely to continue throughout the twenty-first century as science reveals more about physical and biological processes such as global warming, viral replication, and electrical conductivity, and as people apply that new knowledge to personal decisions and government policy. Already, for example, an international treaty calls for immediate reductions in industrial and automobile emissions in response to studies that show a potentially dangerous rise in global temperatures is caused by human activity. Taking an active role in determining the direction of future changes depends on education; people must understand the possible uses of scientific research and the effects of the technology that surrounds them.

The Lucent Books Library of Science and Technology profiles key innovations and discoveries that have transformed the modern world. Each title strives to make a complex scientific discovery, technology, or phenomenon understandable and relevant to the reader. Because scientific discovery is rarely straightforward, each title explains the dead ends, fortunate accidents, and basic scientific methods by which the research into the subject proceeded. And every book examines the practical applications of an invention, branch of science, or scientific principle in industry, public health, and personal life, as well as potential future uses and effects based on ongoing research. Fully documented quotations, annotated bibliographies that include both print and electronic sources, glossaries, indexes, and technical illustrations are among the supplemental features designed to point researchers to further exploration of the subject.

The Age
of Genetics

Journalists have designated the twenty-first century the Age of Genetics. Almost every day, the media carry at least one story about breakthroughs in this fast-growing field. Unlike other science news that is often buried on the back pages, genetics competes with politics and economics for front-page attention. For example, during one thirty-day period toward the end of 2001, the *New York Times* carried twenty-eight major news stories and commentary pieces on advances in genetics and related areas of study.

More dramatically, on a single day, April 12, 2002, three stories reporting the results of groundbreaking genetic discoveries appeared in the nation's newspapers. The headlines that accompanied these articles in one U.S. daily paper reflect the scope of the impact genetics is having on our understanding both of ourselves and the world around us: "Humans, chimps have 98.7% of same genes," "Genes may hold keys to slowing aging," and "Tweak lets tomatoes stay fresh longer."[1]

In its assessment of the most significant events in science in 2001, the magazine *Science News* found that genetics ranked first, playing a key role in forty-eight advances. Astronomy was a distant second with only twenty-six. Statistics from the National Science Foundation reveal that genetics-based research receives more funding, both from government and private investors, than any other branch of science. The field also attracts more college graduate students than any other except computer science and information technology.

Why all the interest? Genetics promises to bring about dramatic changes in almost every area of life: the cure and prevention of disease, the extension of the human life span, the modification of food crops to feed the world's hungry, improved intelligence quotients, more rigorous law enforcement, laboratory-grown replacement organs and other body parts, even the designing of babies to specifications determined by parents, and the cloning of genetically identical copies of individuals. Many of these changes are obviously welcome. However, many are controversial, challenging deeply held religious convictions and moral principles about how far humans should intervene in processes that, until now, have been deemed the exclusive sphere of God or nature.

Hungry children wait for aid in famine-ravaged Africa. Starving people worldwide could be helped by the genetic modification of crops to make food more plentiful and more nutritious.

Early History of Genetics

Genetics is a relatively new science. It rests on two lines of research. The first is the discovery, made in the mid–nineteenth century, of how traits or characteristics (eye color or the susceptibility to a certain disease, for example) are passed from one generation of an organism to another. The second is twentieth-century biochemistry, which made great strides in explaining how cells function to create larger physical structures, like organs, limbs, and even entire individuals. About fifty years ago, these two separate sciences came together to produce modern genetics.

But if the science of genetics is a recent development, the curiosity that inspired it dates back to the beginning of civilization, when the economic basis of human existence shifted from hunting and gathering to agriculture. Primitive farmers noticed that when two varieties of the same plant were grown close to each other, a third type—exhibiting some of the characteristics of the first two—often took root. Farmers who raised animals realized that breeding two hardy specimens together could sometimes result in offspring that were bigger and stronger than either of their parents.

Early humans also knew that some traits tended to run in families. Tall parents often had children who grew up to be tall. Other observable traits also suggested a link between parent and child: basic body type, eye and hair color, even mental and emotional qualities like aggressiveness and passivity. From time to time, traits were observed to skip generations. Children might resemble their grandparents rather than their parents, for example.

Interestingly, most theories that attempted to explain this wealth of observational information were drastically inaccurate. In hindsight, some of these ideas appear not merely wrong, but bizarre. Based on secondhand reports, the ancient Greek philosopher Aristotle concluded that if a camel mated with a leopard, the female would give birth to a giraffe. We now know that this is impossible (species are differentiated from one another by their inability to breed successfully), but to Aristotle and other early thinkers, it was logical to reason that traits from each parent animal would combine to produce uniquely different offspring.

The First Breakthrough

Another theory, which had its supporters until well into the nineteenth century, held that parental traits were blended in children. This notion implies, among other things, that all the children of a tall father and short mother would be of medium height. In fact, the evidence contradicts this assertion. The children of such parents can be tall, short, and intermediate in height. That the theory survived as long as it did in the face of contradictory evidence reflects the general state of confusion about the subject matter of genetics.

The intellectual climate was also influenced by religion, which held that every creature, human and nonhuman, was formed by God. This devoutly held belief gave rise to competing theories, which also had adherents well into the nineteenth century. The first of these held that every child existed in miniature form in his or her father's sperm. The second differed only in asserting that the location of the tiny, fully formed individual was the mother's egg. After the invention of the microscope around the year 1590, a number of scientists claimed to have seen these minuscule entities, called homunculi, through magnifying lenses.

Such was the state of speculation about genetics in 1865, when an eastern European monk named Gregor Mendel published the results of a series of experiments he had conducted on garden peas. Mendel concluded that the traits he observed in his pea plants—height, color, pod shape, and several others—were the result neither of a blend of parental characteristics nor of any preformed microscopic entity residing in the seeds he planted. Rather, Mendel said, these traits were caused by independent "factors"—one factor for each trait— passed down from generation to generation. Today, we call these factors genes.

Although future experiments would prove Mendel correct, he offered no explanation for how these factors produced the traits he observed. Partly for that reason, and partly because he was an obscure researcher and not a leading scientist, his work was ignored until 1900, when the paper he had written thirty-five years earlier was re-discovered by Dutch plant expert Hugo de Vries. Along with two other botanists, de Vries re-created Mendel's experiments and in so doing gave birth to the modern science of genetics.

Gregor Mendel performed a series of experiments on garden peas in the mid–nineteenth century. His findings laid the foundation for the study of genetics.

The Discovery of DNA

By then, chemists and biologists had come to a much more detailed understanding of the structure of cells, the building blocks of all living organisms, than existed in Mendel's day. In 1902, a link was established between chromosomes, large molecular structures in cells, and the inheritance of traits.

For a time, chromosomes were thought to be the "factors" that Mendel had written about, but in 1944, American geneticist Oswald Avery realized that a complex molecule called deoxyribonucleic acid (DNA) played that role. Two years later, it was realized that DNA, which along with a few other chemical substances makes up the chromosomes, is divided into segments. These segments are the genes that provide the blueprint for an organism's specific characteristics.

There were still a number of mysteries to be solved, however. In 1953, James Watson and Francis Crick discovered the structure of the DNA molecule. It is a spiral composed of two long strands, each of which is a mirror image of the other. This key insight enabled subsequent scientists to explain what Gregor Mendel could not—the chemical process by which genes, hidden deep in the body's cells, provide a pattern or recipe for thousands of different proteins. These proteins, in turn, ensure that each individual organism contains all the organs, limbs, and other physical characteristics that make it what it is. For example, they make a rose a rose rather than an oak tree; a horse a horse rather than a human being.

The importance of Watson's and Crick's discovery cannot be overestimated. Together with Mendel's insight of eighty-eight years earlier—and the work of their contemporary, scientist Rosalind Franklin—it laid the groundwork for the diagnosis and treatment of genetic disease, the feats of genetic engineering, and all the other accomplishments that have made genetics the most intriguing and controversial science of the present age. It also made possible the monumental Human Genome Project, a vast international effort to pinpoint the precise location of every gene on every chromosome in the human body. This research was completed in the year 2003, and it will provide scientists with the tools they need to fully exploit the immense promise—and peril—of genetics.

Chapter 1

Inheritance

In legal terms, *inheritance* describes the wealth that parents leave, or pass on, to their children. In biology, the word refers to the genetic processes by which parents endow their children with specific traits, like height, hair color, eye color, and other characteristics. It is an everyday observation that children tend to resemble their parents in many ways, but it is equally obvious that the resemblance is not a simple one. Tall parents do not always produce tall children; children with blue eyes do not necessarily have parents with blue eyes.

Similarity and Difference

Yet, in humans and all other biological organisms, there are clear similarities between one generation and the next: Dogs always give birth to dogs; acorns always develop into oak trees; when a chicken's egg hatches, an infant chicken—not a duck or an eagle—emerges from the shell. In other words, each species, or type of organism, produces members of the same species. Striking similarities also exist within species. Every normal cat has four legs, humans have two, and spiders have eight. Despite these similarities, no two individuals of the same species (except for identical twins or triplets) are carbon copies of each other.

Genetics is the science that explains these similarities and differences. It even explains those rare and often tragic cases where a member of a species is born with physical abnormalities. It does so through

Members of the same species can look very similar, like these baby chicks, but individuals are rarely exact genetic replicas of each other.

what are called the laws of inheritance. These laws were worked out in the middle years of the nineteenth century by an Austrian monk named Gregor Mendel, who devised them after conducting an extensive series of experiments on garden peas. In the years since Mendel did his work, countless experiments with other types of plants and animals have confirmed that the laws of inheritance apply to even extremely complex biological organisms like human beings.

Although Mendel published the results of his work with peas almost a century and a half ago, his experiments are still regarded as masterpieces of scientific method. "While others . . . pondered the huge complexities and confusions of heredity, Mendel perceived that no one would make any progress until they first identified and worked out the simplest possible cases," says science writer Colin Tudge. "Never, in short, in all of science have experiments been more beautifully conceived and executed. This is not the simplicity of a simple man, but of a genius, who sees the simplicity that lies behind the surface incoherence."[2]

That in essence is what science does. It seeks to find simple rules to explain phenomena that on the surface appear to be very complex. When these rules are confirmed by numerous experiments, they are classified as laws. Most scholars agree that the paper in which Mendel recorded the results of his eight years of work with garden peas remains a completely up-to-date discussion of the laws of heredity. "With peas, the simplest possible case, he worked out the ground rules," Tudge says. "But he knew . . . that most cases were more complicated. He wanted to find rules that were universal. I'm sure he felt in his bones that the rules he derived from peas were universal, and that with a little tweaking they could explain the odd patterns of inheritance in beans and bees and, indeed, in human beings."[3]

Reproduction

Some organisms—bacteria, for example—are made up of just a single cell. These life-forms reproduce by a relatively simple process of cell division. Stimulated by internal chemical processes, the solitary cell divides to produce an exact replica, or clone, of itself. The genes contained in the replica are identical to those in the original. Depending on the type of organism involved and the environment in which it is living, cell division can recur a virtually limitless number of times, creating countless identical living things.

However, plants and animals—including human beings—reproduce sexually. That is, genetic material from both a male and a female parent is required to produce a new member of the species. One of the consequences of sexual reproduction and the transfer of genetic information that it entails is that offspring are different from their parents and from each other. Every individual produced in this way, except for identical twins and triplets, is unique.

To arrive at the principles underlying the transmission of traits from parents to their offspring in sexual reproduction, Mendel chose to study garden peas. He focused on seven traits that were easy to observe and, in garden peas, come in two distinct varieties: (1) seed shape, which is either round or wrinkled; (2) seed color, yellow or green; (3) flower color, purple or white; (4) pod shape, inflated or pinched; (5) pod color, green or yellow; (6) stem height, tall or short; and (7) flower position, at the end of the stem or off to the sides.

In order to fully appreciate the laws of inheritance, it is necessary to understand that plants, like people, have male and female sexual organs. However, unlike in people, both sex organs can occur on the same plant. This allows the plant to fertilize itself as well as be cross-fertilized by another plant. The sex organs are located in the flower of the plant. The male organs, called the anthers, produce pollen, which contains the male sex cells, or sperm. When fertilization occurs, pollen is transferred from the anthers to the female organ, called the stigma, where it combines with a female sex cell, or egg.

Mendel's Experiments

In nature, cross-fertilization (also called crossbreeding) occurs when a bee or other insect (or even the wind) transfers pollen from one plant to another. Mendel used a small brush to accomplish this chore. He set himself the task of cross-fertilizing plants with contrasting traits—tall with short, yellow-seeded with green-seeded, and so on—and tabulating the results. He realized that he would have to observe a large number of crossbreedings to compensate for the possibility that some of the results might be due to flukes like unintended wind-borne fertilization. By the time his eight-year experiment was over, he had carefully recorded the results of twenty-eight thousand crossbreedings.

As further insurance against false results, he also made sure that the plants he started with were pure-breeding, another way of saying that for generations they had produced only one version of each of the traits he was interested in. "He had a bunch of plants with yellow seeds that produced only plants with yellow seeds when bred to each other," explains geneticist R. Scott Hawley. "Similarly, he had a bunch of plants with green seeds that produced only plants with green seeds when bred to each other."[4]

When Mendel looked at the first generation of plants produced by his pairings, he found immediate confirmation of his belief that the blending theory of heredity was wrong. The first trait he looked at was seed shape. All the plants produced by crossbreeding round-seed and wrinkle-seed plants had round seeds. Similarly, the mating of tall plants with short ones produced plants that were all tall. There were no intermediate specimens—no seeds that were somewhat

Seven Traits Observed by Mendel

PEA PLANTS

Trait	Variety
Seed Shape	Round or Wrinkled
Seed Color	Green or Yellow
Flower Color	Purple or White
Flower Position	End of Stem or off to the Sides
Pod Shape	Inflated or Pinched
Pod Color	Green or Yellow
Stem Height	Tall or Short

wrinkled and no plants whose height fell between that of its tall and short parents.

Discussing seed color, Hawley says,

> In the first generation, when Mendel crossed plants with green seeds to plants with yellow seeds, all he saw in the progeny were plants with seeds identical in color to those of the green-seeded parent. It didn't matter which way the cross was made (i.e., green males crossed to yellow females or vice versa), all the offspring had green seeds. . . . A real adherent to blending would have postulated that the progeny of the first generation should have been yellowish-green, not true green.[5]

One Gene, Two Variants

This part of Mendel's experiment established the first principle of inheritance. If genetic material was not blended, then it had to be passed on in discrete units. These units—Mendel called them factors, but they are now referred to as genes—retained their individual identity in the newly created organisms, which could then pass them on to succeeding generations. The second, and equally important, principle of inheritance came to light when Mendel bred second-generation plants to themselves and each other. Traits—yellow seeds and shortness, for example—that had vanished in the second generation suddenly reappeared in the third.

With respect to height, one out of every four third-generation plants was short. Mendel obtained similar ratios for the other traits he was studying. "In the subsequent generation, green-seeded plants crossed to themselves or each other produced both yellow and green-seeded plants," Hawley explains.

> In order to explain differences in traits, Mendel supposed that genes could take different forms, called alleles, that specified different expressions of

the trait. For example, Mendel claimed that there was a gene that gave seed color and two different forms or alleles of that gene: one specifying green color and one specifying yellow color.

In addition, an individual must be able to carry genetic information for a trait it does not express. (We know that the green-seeded progeny [offspring] produced by the first generation carried the information to produce yellow seeds because they were able to pass it on to the yellow-seeded progeny in the next generation.) Mendel's second insight was that this pattern of inheritance could only be explained if the green alleles could mask the expression of the yellow alleles, such that individuals getting a green allele from mom and a yellow allele from dad would be just as green as those that got green alleles, and only green alleles, from both parents. . . . To denote this difference between the ability of alleles to determine a [trait], Mendel introduced the terms dominant and recessive.[6]

That every gene comes in two varieties, a dominant form and a recessive form, explains the ability of traits to skip generations. Each parent passes on one allele of each gene to each child. A child who inherits two dominant alleles for a given trait will exhibit that trait. A child who inherits one dominant and one recessive allele will also exhibit the trait because the dominant allele will mask the presence of the recessive allele. Only if the child inherits two recessive alleles will the dominant trait not appear.

Dominant and Recessive Traits

The propensity for red hair, for example, could be lurking in recessive form in the genes two nonredheaded parents pass along to their children. Those children will, in turn, pass it on to their children. Should one of those children grow up and marry someone also carrying the recessive form of the gene, and should they both pass on the recessive form to their offspring, redheadedness will suddenly emerge after an absence of several generations in the family tree.

The height of garden pea plants illustrates this point clearly. With respect to the gene that governs this trait, the dominant allele leads to tallness and the recessive allele leads to shortness. A pea plant will be tall if it inherits the dominant (tall) allele of the gene from each of its parent plants. It will also be tall if it inherits one dominant (tall) allele and one

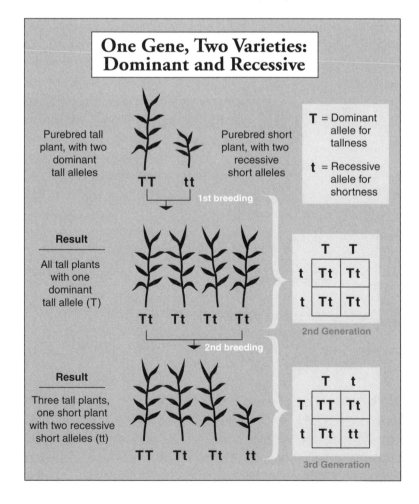

One Gene, Two Varieties: Dominant and Recessive

Purebred tall plant, with two dominant tall alleles

TT

Purebred short plant, with two recessive short alleles

tt

T = Dominant allele for tallness

t = Recessive allele for shortness

1st breeding

Result

All tall plants with one dominant tall allele (T)

Tt   Tt   Tt   Tt

	T	T
t	Tt	Tt
t	Tt	Tt

2nd Generation

2nd breeding

Result

Three tall plants, one short plant with two recessive short alleles (tt)

TT   Tt   Tt   tt

	T	t
T	TT	Tt
t	Tt	tt

3rd Generation

recessive (short) allele. Only if it inherits two recessive alleles will it be short.

This insight is one of the cornerstones of modern genetics: Rather than blending in offspring, genes are inherited from parents as discrete units that come in two forms, each of which is passed on separately and remains separate in the genetic makeup of the new individual. This means that recessive traits can be passed on from generation to generation without leaving a visible trail.

"Mendel concluded that the hereditary determinants for the traits in the parental lines were transmitted as two different elements that retain their purity in the hybrids [the plants resulting from crossbreeding]," says geneticist Daniel L. Hartl. "In other words, the hereditary determinants do not 'mix' or 'contaminate each other.' The implication of this conclusion is that a plant with the dominant trait might carry, in unchanged form, a hereditary determinant for the recessive trait."[7]

Segregation and Assortment

In humans, for example, a dimpled chin is caused by a dominant allele. A person with a dimpled chin has either one or two dominant alleles for this trait. The absence of a dimple indicates that two recessive alleles are present in the person's genetic makeup. However, since someone with a dimpled chin might have a recessive allele for that trait, it is possible for that person to pass it on to a child. Should that child's other parent also contribute a recessive allele for this trait, the child would have a dimpled chin.

This property of genes, that they each come in two different forms or alleles and that each parent contributes one allele to the genetic makeup of his or her children, is called the principle of segregation. Support for this principle came in the twentieth century when biologists discovered that when sex cells—male sperm and female eggs—are formed, each carries

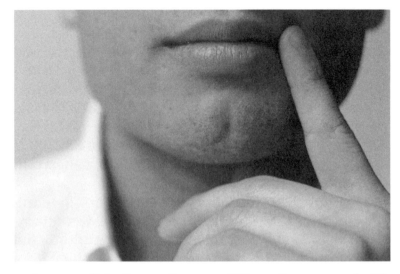

only one allele for each gene. When the sperm fertilizes the egg to form a new individual, these alleles recombine and, according to the rules of dominance and recessiveness, produce the traits the new individual exhibits. Each egg cell and each sperm cell are just as likely to contain one allele as they are to contain the other.

Another important law of inheritance, also discovered by Mendel and proved by subsequent research, is called the principle of independent assortment. In conducting his experiments with peas, Mendel noticed that traits were inherited independently of each other. In other words, whether a plant was tall or short had no effect on whether its seeds were green or yellow. This is because the traits he was looking at are caused by genes that are located on different chromosomes (structures in each of an organism's cells). Mendel was not in a position to know this fact, but it was proved when the structure of cells was determined in the decades after he completed his work.

Exceptions to Mendel's Rules

While it is true that Mendel's description of the principles of genetic inheritance has been confirmed by tens of thousands of experiments on plants and animals, it is also true that the transmission of genetic information from one generation to another is somewhat more complex than he realized. In certain cases, called incomplete dominance, the inheritance of both a dominant and a recessive allele of a gene does produce what appears to be a blend of traits.

Certain flowers, for example, come in three colors. When a dominant and a recessive allele for the gene that determines color combine, the result is a shade intermediate between the two other colors that the flower can assume. Although this seems to suggest that a blending of genetic material has occurred, it has not. It is simply a property of these flowers' genes to produce three colors and not two, as Mendel's peas did.

Another subtlety that escaped Mendel has come to be known as quantitative inheritance. The traits he studied were very easy to observe: A seed was either green or yellow, a plant was either tall or short. Each of these traits was caused by a single gene. Some characteristics, however, do not lend themselves so easily to either-or classification. Human skin color, to take an obvious example, comes in a wide range of shades. Scientists now know that these traits are determined by more than one gene. It is the combined effect of all the relevant genes that produce the characteristic, allowing for more variation than occurs when only single genes are involved.

The rules of inheritance that Mendel discovered—that genetic material is passed from generation to generation in discrete units, that these units come in two forms called alleles, that each parent contributes one allele for each gene to the offspring, and that the units operate independently of each other—laid the groundwork for twentieth-century genetics. From his modest experiments with garden peas have come the breakthroughs that are revolutionizing biological science and our understanding of life itself.

Chapter 2

Genes and DNA

In order to understand why the laws of inheritance work as they do, scientists had to look into the interior of cells. Cells are the building blocks of life, and all living things—from bacteria to human beings—are composed of them. The number of cells varies greatly from organism to organism: A bacterium has just one cell; an average-sized adult human has between 60 trillion and 100 trillion. Most cells are too small to be seen with the naked eye and must be viewed under a microscope. In the human body, almost all cells vary between $\frac{1}{25,000}$ of an inch and $\frac{1}{125,000}$ of an inch in diameter, although there is a nerve cell in the upper leg that, while extremely thin, is several feet long. Other cells are larger. A hen's egg, for example, is a single cell, and the largest cell of any organism on Earth is the ostrich egg, which weighs about a pound. Even the smallest cell contains a complete copy of the genetic information that gives an individual organism the traits that make it what it is and not some other thing. Cells have what are called life cycles. They are created, live, reproduce, and die. It is during the process of reproduction, or cell division, that genetic information is passed along from generation to generation.

Simple and Complex Cells

There are two types of cells, prokaryotes and eukaryotes. (The words are pronounced "pro-carry-oats" and "you-carry-oats.") Prokaryotes are the kind of cells of which bacteria and other single-celled organisms are composed. More complex forms of life, including plants and animals, are made of many eukaryotes. The two types of cells are distinguished from each other by their internal structure. Both are enclosed within an external membrane that separates them from their environment. All the internal components of a prokaryote float within this membrane. Eukaryotes, on the other hand, have a number of additional internal membranes that divide them into compartments.

The principal compartments of a eukaryotic cell are the nucleus and the cytoplasm. To use an analogy from the world of business, the nucleus is the cell's executive office and the cytoplasm is its factory. The nucleus generates instructions for a number of cellular processes that are, in turn, carried out in the cytoplasm. The nucleus of a eukaryotic cell is itself a complex structure. It is composed of DNA (deoxyribonucleic acid), which contains genetic information and

Single-celled bacteria infect a host. These organisms are far simpler creatures than their multicelled counterparts.

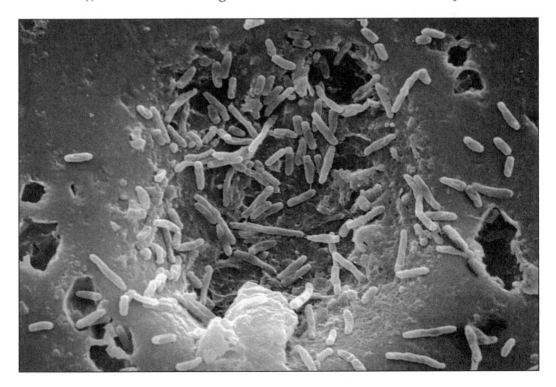

combines with proteins to produce a substance called chromatin.

"Throughout most of the life cycle of the cell, chromatin exists as exceedingly long, thin, entangled threads that cannot be clearly distinguished by any microscope," says geneticist William K. Purves.

> However, when the nucleus is about to divide, the chromatin condenses and coils tightly to form a precise number of readily visible objects called chromosomes. Each chromosome contains one long molecule of DNA. The chromosomes are the bearers of hereditary instructions; their DNA carries the information required to perform the functions of the cell and endow the cell's descendants with the same instructions.[8]

The number of chromosomes in each cell varies from organism to organism, but they always come in matched pairs called homologues. Human beings have 23 pairs of chromosomes for a total of 46. Chimpanzees, humanity's closest relative in the animal kingdom, have 24 pairs; dogs have 39; cats, 17; ferns, 256. Thus, in humans, the genetic information contained in DNA is divided among 23 pairs of homologous (matching) chromosomes in such a way that the nucleus of each individual cell contains a complete copy of the organism's entire genetic code. Each chromosome is a long molecule which is further divided into subsections of genetic information. These subsections are the factors that Mendel discovered—what today we call genes.

Chromosomes, DNA, and Genes

Although the chromosomes contain a copy of an individual's genetic makeup—all the genes necessary to produce all the individual's traits—the two members of each matching set of chromosomes are not exactly identical to each other. This is because one set of chromosomes is inherited from the maternal

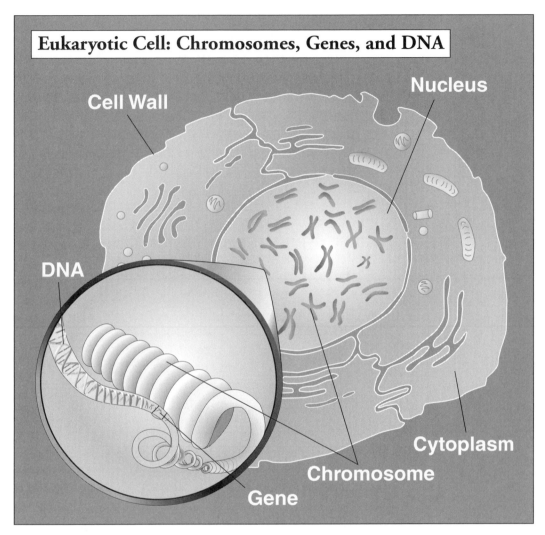

Eukaryotic Cell: Chromosomes, Genes, and DNA

Cell Wall

Nucleus

DNA

Cytoplasm

Chromosome

Gene

parent and its matching partner from the paternal parent. Thus, it is possible for homologous chromosomes to contain different alleles for the same gene. In Mendel's experiments with peas, with respect to height some of his plants contained two dominant alleles for tallness, some contained two recessive alleles for shortness, and some contained both a dominant and recessive allele.

This fact is crucial for an understanding of genetic inheritance. It explains why children are not identical to one or the other of their parents. It also explains why parents can pass on the genes for recessive traits, traits that they do not themselves exhibit, to their progeny and why a specific trait may lie dormant for generations before making its appearance in a family tree. That matching homologous chromosomes can contain different alleles for the same gene accounts for the pervasive fact of genetic diversity—how from a relatively limited number of genes a virtually unlimited number of unique individuals can be produced.

Science writer Laura Gould sums up the role of the cell nucleus and its contents in the production of the traits that distinguish one individual from another:

> Chromosomes are thread-like structures in the nucleus of almost every cell [some red blood cells don't have a nucleus]; they are made in part of DNA. They come in matching pairs, one member of the pair providing genetic information from the mother, the other from the father. . . . Genes are just little pieces of chromosomes: tiny segments of DNA. . . . Each gene has a fixed location on its chromosome and helps to specify a trait.[9]

Genes determine traits because they function as a code that tells structures in the cytoplasm how to function. The cytoplasm is found outside the cell's nucleus. A computer analogy is useful: The DNA contained in genes performs like software, telling the hardware in the cytoplasm what to do. Specifically, it sends a message through the membrane that encloses the nucleus to entities called ribosomes in the cytoplasm to manufacture one or several of a wide range of proteins. It is these proteins that actually do the work of making peas tall or short, or humans brown-eyed or blue-eyed.

The Genetic Alphabet

DNA was discovered in 1869 by a German scientist named Friedrich Miescher. He found it while studying pus that had accumulated on the bandages of wounded soldiers. Miescher, along with other scientists, learned that DNA was a large molecule composed mostly of a type of sugar called deoxyribose, which is related to table sugar. They also found traces of phosphate, a chemical derived from the element phosphorous. But the most important discovery was that DNA also contained four substances called nucleotide bases. These bases are adenosine, cytosine, guanine, and thymine, and they are abbreviated A, C, G, and T.

Miescher suspected that these bases combined to form chemical messages, and in so doing he came close to discovering the genetic code that governs all life. In fact, later research has shown that the bases that compose DNA function exactly like an alphabet that encodes meaningful expressions. In the same way that the twenty-six letters of the English alphabet can be combined to form an enormous number of intelligible words, phrases, and sentences, the four letters of the genetic alphabet—A, C, G, and T—combine with each other to create chemical messages that are then transmitted to the ribosomes and other parts of the cell.

However, for a language to work as a method of communication, the various letters have to be associated with each other according to a set of rules. In human languages, these rules are called grammar and syntax. The genetic code also has a set of rules, but it took scientists a long time to discover exactly what it was. The first clue came in the early part of the twentieth century when they found that in any DNA molecule the number of As must equal the number of Ts and the number of Cs must equal the number of Gs, but the number of A-T, C-G combinations does not have to be equal.

The importance of this piece of information, however, was not understood for almost fifty years until scientists developed a complete description of how the various components of a DNA molecule fit together. This feat was accomplished by a process called X-ray crystallography, in which a substance is combined with salt and allowed to form crystals. When these crystals are viewed under a powerful electron microscope, the structure of molecules becomes apparent. However, electron microscopes do not produce precise visual images of what they are focused on. Instead, they generate data that have to be interpreted.

The Structure of DNA

In the 1940s, two British scientists, Rosalind Franklin and Maurice Wilkins, applied the techniques of X-ray crystallography to DNA. Two other scientists, American geneticist James Watson and British bio-

James Watson (left) and Francis Crick study their DNA model. Watson and Crick were the first scientists to construct a physical model of the DNA molecule.

physicist Francis Crick, became aware of their work and began to construct a physical model of the DNA molecule. The 1953 paper in which Watson and Crick published the results of their painstaking research has been recognized as one of the most revolutionary and influential documents in the history of science.

Watson, Crick, and Wilkins each received a Nobel Prize for their work. Unfortunately, Franklin died before her invaluable contribution could be recognized in this way. Recently, historians of science have finally begun to recognize that without Franklin's groundbreaking work, the discovery of the structure of the DNA molecule would have been delayed by years, if not decades.

Watson and Crick concluded that the DNA molecule was shaped like a double helix, two strands spiraling around each other. Former *New York Times* science editor Boyce Rensberger explains:

> A helix is the shape of a corkscrew. A double helix is the shape of two corkscrews, one intertwined with the other and curving parallel to it, like the railings of a spiral staircase. Another way to think of the double helix is to imagine a twisted rope ladder with rigid rungs, each rope forming a helix. The easiest way to think about DNA is to start by splitting the two helices [the plural form of the word *helix*] apart. Think of it as sawing down through the middles of the wooden rungs of a rope ladder. The result is two single ropes with half-rungs hanging off each rope.[10]

Watson and Crick's discovery of the double helix structure of DNA unlocked the secret of the rules that govern the genetic code. In every DNA molecule each A is associated with a T and each C with a G. "In all DNA the rope part of the ladder is the same up and down its length—a monotonous alteration of sugar and phosphate molecules," Rensberger continues.

"The half-rungs, which stick out from the sugars, are the interesting parts. They serve as the four letters of the genetic alphabet. . . . As in the English language, the sequence of bases along one strand of DNA—the sequence of As, Ts, Cs, and Gs—spells out the genetic message. . . . Opposite every T would be an A (and vice versa) and opposite every G would be a C (and vice versa)."[11] Extending the comparison between the genetic code and human language, a gene, as a sequence of As, Ts, Cs, and Gs along the entwined strands of DNA that make up a chromosome, becomes the equivalent of a sentence.

The question then arises: How can just four letters create code for the thousands of proteins that the body produces and the correspondingly large number of traits they govern? The answer lies in the astonishingly large number of A-T, C-G combinations, or base pairs as they are called, that make up a gene. If all the DNA compacted into a cell were stretched out, it would be about seven feet long. Thus, says R. Scott Hawley, "The average human DNA molecule is 65 million base pairs in length for a total DNA content of six trillion base pairs."[12] So, although the four genetic letters can be put together in only a few unique ways, the fact that each pairing on the 6 million rungs of the DNA ladder can be different from creature to creature or plant to plant accounts for the complexity of life.

DNA and RNA

The sequences of DNA that make up genes communicate instructions to the ribosomes to manufacture proteins that work together to produce an organism's traits. However, genes do not perform this function directly. First, a process called transcription must occur. In transcription, a single gene, which could contain thousands of base pairs, unravels from the chromosome on which it is located. The DNA that constitutes that gene then splits into its two complementary strands. A special type of protein called an enzyme moves along one of the strands letter by letter and creates a corresponding strand of a substance called ribonucleic acid (RNA).

RNA is similar to DNA in that it that it has four nucleotide bases. Three of these bases—A, C, and G—are the same in both, but in place of thymine (T), RNA has a base called uracil, which is abbreviated with the letter U. As the enzyme creeps along the gene's DNA, it transcribes each base it encounters into a corresponding base on the newly emerging strand of RNA. Thus, a C on the DNA strand becomes a G on the RNA strand, a G becomes a C, a T becomes an A, but the As are transcribed not into Ts but into Us. For example, a strand of DNA that reads ACGGCAT would be transcribed as UGC-CGUA.

Once the strand of RNA has been completely transcribed, it travels through the membrane that encloses the cell's nucleus into the cytoplasm. There, it attaches itself to a ribosome, providing the instructions needed to manufacture a protein. This process is called translation, and it works like this. The thousands of proteins that any organism

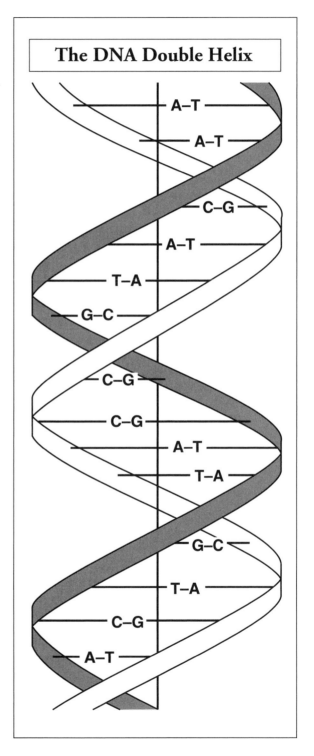

The DNA Double Helix

A–T
A–T
C–G
A–T
T–A
G–C
C–G
C–G
A–T
T–A
G–C
T–A
C–G
A–T

contains are made up of various combinations of twenty substances called amino acids. Each three-letter sequence of RNA tells the ribosome to make one of these amino acids. The process continues in sequence, each three letters of RNA bringing into existence a new amino acid, which attaches itself to those already made. At the conclusion of the process, a complete protein has been manufactured and is ready to do its part in producing the traits that characterize the organism in which all this activity has been taking place.

The three-letter sequence of RNA that codes for an amino acid is called a condon. Together, the condons form a set of instructions—the genetic code mentioned earlier. This code is the basis for all the forms that life can take. It bridges the gap between the hereditary information that genes contain and the biochemical processes that give each individual organism the traits that define it.

Mitosis

The way genes encode instructions for the manufacture of proteins is similar to the mechanism they use to pass from generation to generation. A key part of the life cycle of every cell takes place when the cell reproduces, or makes a copy of itself. Eukaryotic cells, those that make up complex organisms like plants and animals, come in two types. These types are somatic cells and sex cells, also called gametes. Somatic cells combine with each other to make up a body's tissues and organs. Sex cells combine with the sex cells of another organism to produce offspring.

The two sorts of eukaryotes reproduce in different ways. When somatic cells divide, they include a complete copy of all the genetic information contained in the original cell. That is, both corresponding sets of chromosomes are replicated in the new cell. On the other hand, when sex cells divide, only one of the two sets of chromosomes is reproduced. When the sex cell combines with the opposite sex cell of another organism—a sperm cell with an egg cell—the new cell produced by this union will then contain two matching sets of chromosomes, but one will have come from the father and the other will have come from the mother.

The reproduction of somatic cells is called mitosis; that of sex cells is termed meiosis. The purpose of mitosis is growth, so that organs and other body parts can form completely as an organism progresses from infancy to adulthood. Mitosis also creates new cells to replace those that die off at the end of their life cycles. The purpose of meiosis is to create an entirely new organism.

Compared to meiosis, mitosis is a relatively straightforward process. First, the chromosomes become thicker and double into cross-shaped forms, each limb of the cross containing a complete copy of the DNA in all of the organism's genes. Biochemists Paul Berg and Maxine Singer describe how the phenomenon continues: "All of the chromosomes eventually line up in the central plane of the cell and then divide into two groups; the two groups then move to opposite ends of the cell. Two cells are formed when a membrane grows and separates the two ends of the original cell. Each of the new cells (referred to as daughter cells) has a full set of chromosome pairs."[13]

Meiosis

Because sex cells combine to form a new organism, they cannot each have a full complement of matching chromosomes. If they did, the offspring resulting from the union of two sex cells would have twice the number of chromosomes—and twice the amount of genetic information—as either of the two parent cells. In humans, for example, each child would have not the required forty-six chromosomes but two times that number, or ninety-two. Human offspring with more or less than the necessary forty-six chromosomes usually do not survive; consequently the human race would have died out after the first generation.

Therefore, sex cells divide twice. The first division is like mitosis, except that during the stage when the number of chromosomes doubles, individual genes often jump from one chromosome to the other. This is possible because similar genes occur at the same location on each of the chromosomes. The process, known as crossing over or recombination, plays a

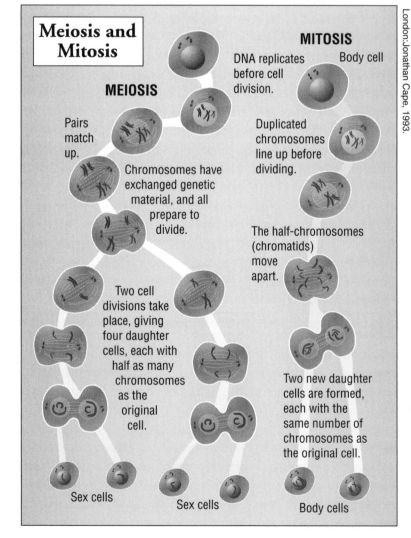

Meiosis and Mitosis

MEIOSIS

Pairs match up.

Chromosomes have exchanged genetic material, and all prepare to divide.

Two cell divisions take place, giving four daughter cells, each with half as many chromosomes as the original cell.

Sex cells

Sex cells

MITOSIS

DNA replicates before cell division.

Body cell

Duplicated chromosomes line up before dividing.

The half-chromosomes (chromatids) move apart.

Two new daughter cells are formed, each with the same number of chromosomes as the original cell.

Body cells

Source: Colin Tudge, *The Engineer in the Garden: Genes and Genetics: From the Idea of Heredity to the Creation of Life*. London: Jonathan Cape, 1993.

key role in genetic engineering and also promotes genetic diversity. Since one member of each pair of chromosomes has been inherited from the mother and the other from the father and since each gene has two forms (alleles), recombination creates a novel arrangement of genetic information to be passed on to future generations.

Once the chromosomes have doubled and two new cells have been formed, a further division takes place to guarantee that each sex cell produced has only one set of chromosomes (in humans, twenty-three rather than forty-six). "These two paired sets of recombined chromosomes now separate in the phase known as meiosis-II, or reduction division," says Colin Tudge. "Without further doubling of chromosome material, each pair of chromosomes from each set separates from its homologue [matching partner]. Meiosis results in four cells, each . . . containing just one set of chromosomes, and each of those chromosomes is a unique new entity, combining genetic material from both parents."[14]

When each individual sex cell meets up with its partner of the opposite sex during reproduction, a new cell is formed that contains the chromosomes, and the recombined genes on those chromosomes, from each of the parent cells. Thus a new creature is created. It is similar to its parents because it has the same genes as they did, but it is also different because each of those genes may contain alleles different from the ones that constituted the genetic makeup of the parents. As this process continues from generation to generation, the individuals produced tend to differ to an ever-greater degree from the original parent pair. These differences enable subsequent generations to adapt to changing environment and form the genetic basis of evolution, explaining how species have changed, and new species have arisen, during the course of the history of life on Earth.

Whether a human embryo develops into a male or a female is determined by the chromosomes it inherits from its parents.

Sex Determination

There is one exception to the rule that all chromosomes come in matching pairs, and that exception determines whether newly conceived organisms develop into males or females. The pair of dissimilar chromosomes have been designated X and Y. It is important to remember that although they have different names, they do form a pair in the same way their more alike counterparts do. The Y chromosome is shorter than the X. That is just another way of saying that it has fewer genes, or less genetic material. But it does contain one gene that the X does not, and that is the TDF gene—the gene that causes maleness.

Every normal human female has two X chromosomes; every normal male has both an X and a Y. (There are variations to this rule in some other types of organisms.) When eggs, the female sex cells, are formed during the first stage of meiosis, each one gets two copies of the X chromosome. When sperm cells are formed, each gets an X and a Y. When these cells divide again during the second stage of meiosis to create a cell with only one copy of each chromosome, the egg must have an X and only an X because that is all it had to start with. A sperm cell can have either an X or a Y.

When egg and sperm combine during the conception of a new individual, the cell that is produced must therefore inherit one X chromosome from its mother. From its father, however, it can inherit either an X or a Y. Whether a sperm cell has an X or a Y chromosome is random, accounting for the roughly equal number of males and females born.

For the first six weeks of life, the human embryo, whether it is to become a male or female, develops in the same way. Sometime during the seventh or eighth week of pregnancy, the TDF gene provided by the Y chromosome, if there is one, becomes active. During this period of activity, which lasts only during this phase of the embryo's growth, the gene sends chemical instructions to other genes, telling them to produce the proteins that will cause certain cells to mature into male testicles. The testicles produce hormones which create other male sexual characteristics. If only X chromosomes are present, this process does not occur and the embryo develops into a female.

Chapter 3

Genetic Engineering

Genes contain coded information that leads to the production of proteins. Proteins, in turn, are responsible for creating the traits that characterize individual organisms. Therefore, if a way could be found to transfer genes from one organism to another, creatures could be manufactured with traits that they had never before exhibited. Based on the description of the structure of DNA provided by Watson and Crick, researchers began to search for a way to cut genes from the DNA of one organism and paste them into another. By the 1970s, they had the answer, and the science of genetic engineering was born. It was a giant step forward. Now, a mere thirty years later, it is possible to exchange genes between one plant and another and one animal and another. It is even possible to transpose genes between plants and animals. No organism—from primitive life-forms, like bacteria, to higher order animals, like human beings—is exempt from this genetic swap meet. Genetic engineering has led to monumental advances in medicine and agriculture, but it has also given rise to a storm of controversy and debate over the limits on humankind's intrusion into the natural order of things.

Restriction Enzymes and Plasmids

The first major breakthrough on the road to genetic engineering came with work done on restriction endonucleases by Herbert Boyer of the University of California at San Francisco. As defined by Karl Drlica in *Understanding DNA and Gene Cloning: A Guide for the Curious*, restriction endonucleases "are a group of enzymes [a special type of protein] that . . . occur naturally in a large number of different bacterial species, serving as part of the natural defense mechanism that protects bacterial cells against invasion by foreign DNA molecules such as those contained in viruses."[15]

When, for example, a virus attacks a single-celled bacterium, restriction endonucleases are unleashed and go to work, cutting the invading DNA into small, nonthreatening pieces. "Crucial to this protective device is the ability of the nuclease to discriminate between its own DNA and the invading DNA; otherwise the cell would destroy its own DNA," Drlica says.

> This recognition process involves two elements. First there are specific nucleotide sequences [As and Ts, Cs and Gs] that act as targets for the nuclease. These are called the restriction sites. Second, there is a protective chemical signal that can be placed by the cell on all the target sequences that happen to occur in its own DNA. The signal modifies the DNA and prevents the nuclease from cutting. Invading DNAs, lacking the protective signal, would be chopped by the nuclease.[16]

Thus, restriction enzymes have the remarkable ability to recognize specific arrangements of DNA base pairs—As and Ts, Gs and Cs. They also have the capacity to act like a molecular scalpel, severing the DNA at exactly the spot where they detect this sequence of genetic letters. Restriction enzymes are a powerful tool because there are thousands of them, and each one acts only on a unique arrangement of As and Ts and Cs and Gs.

A second piece of the genetic engineering puzzle fell into place when it was discovered that bacteria

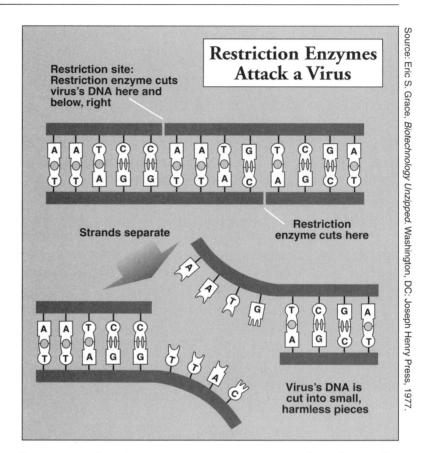

Source: Eric S. Grace, *Biotechnology Unzipped*. Washington, DC: Joseph Henry Press, 1977.

have another interesting property. Under the right conditions, small, circular pieces of DNA can be transferred from one bacterial cell to another. These DNA structures, called plasmids, are not located on the bacterium's solitary chromosome, but float freely in other parts of the organism. Single-cell bacteria duplicate when the cell divides, producing an exact copy of itself. During this process, its plasmids, as well as its chromosomal DNA, are also reproduced. "In 1959, Japanese doctors found that the ineffectiveness of antibiotics as a cure for dysentery with some patients was due to the fact that the bacteria with which the patients were infected carried a plasmid containing several genes of resistance to different antibiotics," says geneticist Maxim D. Frank-Kamenetskii. "It was discovered that genes of resistance to antibiotics are always carried by plasmids. An ability to move freely between bacteria enables the plasmids carrying such genes to spread rapidly among bacteria immediately in the wake of a broad application of the antibiotic."[17]

Recombinant DNA Technology

Boyer and Stanley Cohen, another scientist at the University of California who was working on plasmids, pooled their knowledge to conduct a series of experiments on two different strains of the E. coli bacteria. Some forms of E. coli live in the intestines of humans and other animals, where they aid the body's digestive processes. Boyer and Cohen marshaled restriction endonucleases to cut some E. coli plasmids. When plasmids are cut, they leave what researchers call "sticky ends," to which other plasmid segments can easily attach themselves. The point at which the pieces of the two plasmids join is cemented by the activity of an enzyme called ligase, which can be described as molecular glue, to form a stable chemical bond. Then, the two scientists severed particular genes from another type of bacteria, one that was resistant to antibiotics, and spliced them to the sticky ends of the cut E. coli plasmids. The result: a hybrid form of antibiotic-resistant E. coli.

One big question remained to be answered. Thus far,

Dr. Stanley Cohen was one of two scientists who first experimented with an antibiotic-resistant E. coli hybrid.

genes had been successfully exchanged between two types of bacteria, but would the same cut-and-paste technique work when the genes came from two radically different life-forms? In other words, could genes cross species boundaries? Cohen's and Boyer's first attempt to transplant genes from one form of life into another involved a tadpole and E. coli bacteria. The scientists removed a gene from one of the tadpole's cells and transplanted it into an E. coli bacterial cell. When the bacterial cell started to multiply, the scientists analyzed each successive generation and found that they all contained the tadpole gene. The first gene transfer between species had been accomplished, and the door was now open to a wide range of similar experiments—many of them far more controversial. It had been practically demonstrated that genes from fish, even genes from plants, could be transplanted into humans.

The new technique was called recombinant DNA technology—just another name for genetic engineering—because the procedure recombined genes that originated in different organisms. The popular media gave it another name that has been responsible for a great deal of confusion. They called it gene cloning, creating the belief that science could duplicate entire organisms, an achievement that was not at that point even distantly attainable. But what the technique did allow scientists to do was create specific types of proteins in large quantities. "Usually, a specific protein is produced by a cell in very small quantities, sometimes a mere one or two molecules per cell," says Frank-Kamenetskii.

As a result, the production of proteins needed for particular research was an arduous and costly undertaking. One had to process dozens of kilograms [a unit of weight equal to 2.2 pounds], nay tons, of biomass to obtain milligrams of protein.

Despite such meager quantities, it was still not possible to ensure the necessary purity of the protein. Hence, the cost of many protein preparations was exorbitant and their purity was substandard. Genetic engineering brought about a radical change in this situation. Genetic-engineering strains now exist—superproducers of many proteins with high standards of purity—that were undreamed of before. Molecular biology firms have sharply diversified the production of enzymes and other protein preparations and have reduced the prices of these products. Thus, molecular biology received a powerful new impetus, resulting in an unheard of acceleration in the pace of scientific research.[18]

In accomplishing this goal, bacteria, especially E. coli bacteria, have proved to be the most effective host for transplanted genes because they reproduce rapidly. For example, if scientists wish to produce a certain kind of protein, they snip the required genes from an animal that produces the protein naturally and transplant them into an E. coli cell. They then put the cell in an environment that encourages it to divide and just let nature take its course until they have millions of cells all producing the desired protein. Finally, the scientists extract the protein from the cells and use it for whatever purpose they have in mind.

Biofoods

The first area in which the new science of genetic engineering took hold was agriculture. It quickly became apparent that food plants could be genetically altered so they were more resistant to pests, needed less water to grow, and provided more nutrition than in their natural states. Since human beings first began to till the land, farmers have been trying to produce hardier, more profitable crops. The method

Thanks to advances in genetic engineering, farmers can now crossbreed crops like these corn plants to produce foods that are healthier and hardier than those that grow naturally.

at their disposal was called selective breeding. In the same way that Gregor Mendel bred pea plants to yield other pea plants with certain traits, agriculturists crossbred the healthiest plants with each other to create the most productive varieties possible. But the process took a long time and, because the relationship between genes and traits is complex, often led to unwanted results.

Genetic engineering takes the guesswork out of this effort and greatly reduces the time it takes to produce a plant with the desired traits. It also—for the first time—makes it possible to breed entirely different types or species of plants with each other to create some truly novel hybrids. Previously, selective breeding limited farmers to experiments with plants of the same or very closely related species. By cutting and pasting genes from one plant to another, genetic engineers are able to do all the things that crossbreeding can do, and do them faster and more accurately.

The technique also allows scientists to do things that nature alone is incapable of doing. A report prepared at University of Virginia on the state of currently available genetically engineered, or transgenic, plants states:

> Many plants have been commercialized, including tomatoes and squash and commodity crops like corn and soybeans. Most have been engineered for one of three traits: herbicide [weed killer] tolerance, insect resistance, or virus tolerance. This is the fastest growing area of biotechnology in agriculture. Genetically engineered cotton has been approved for commercial use. There are between 10 and 12 million acres of cotton in the U.S. and estimates are that all of this acreage will be planted to transgenic varieties within the next 10 years. One of the newest innovations in cotton is the development of naturally-colored cotton fibers where the pigments have come from inserting color genes from flowers into cotton.[19]

As a further indication of the widespread use of genetic engineering in farming, the Food and Agriculture Organization of the United Nations, citing figures for the year 1999 (the process of gathering such information accurately is slow when developing countries are involved), reports:

Transgenic plants . . . now cover large areas in certain parts of the world. Estimates for 1999 indicate that 39.9 million hectares [a unit of measurement equivalent to 2.47 acres] were planted with transgenic crops. . . . Of the 39.9 million hectares, 28.1 million (i.e. 71%) were modified for tolerance to a specific herbicide (which could be sprayed on the field, killing weeds while leaving the crop undamaged); 8.9 million hectares (22%) were modified to include a toxin-producing gene from a soil bacterium . . . which poisons insects feeding on the plants, while 2.9 million hectares (7%) were planted with crops having both herbicide tolerance and insect resistance.[20]

The bioengineering of plants has become big business. Hundreds of millions of dollars of research money are being poured into a diverse range of projects. Among the most promising are creating plants that produce their own fertilizer and modifying plants to be delivery systems for medicines and nutrients they do not naturally produce. For example, work is under way to produce a banana that contains in its DNA a vaccine for hepatitis B, a highly contagious disease that damages the livers of people who contract it. The banana is also being turned into a megavitamin to deliver much-needed nutrients to children in the underdeveloped countries of Africa and Asia.

Transgenic Animals

Plants are not the only organisms that genetic engineers are working on. Turning their attention to animals, scientists have produced a number of transgenic creatures they hope will bring major benefits to mankind. For example, human genes have been put into pigs to allow the pigs to produce human insulin, a substance needed to control diabetes, one of the fastest-growing diseases in affluent countries.

The applications are wide-ranging. Goats are being genetically modified to produce a protein that aids in blood clotting. Other experiments with goats aim to find cures for multiple sclerosis and some forms of cancer. Sheep are being altered to generate a protein that may fight the lung disease emphysema. Designer dairy products are also on the drawing boards. Geneticists hope to end up with a breed of cow that produces, for example, only low-fat milk.

Other genetically engineered animals are being designed to contract human diseases so that experimental treatments can be explored. In these cases, healthy genes are replaced with malfunctioning counterparts, using a technique similar to the cut-and-paste procedure used with plasmids.

Finally, researchers are optimistic that they will be able to turn animals, principally pigs, into sources of organs for human transplants. To accomplish this, they are transferring human genes into pigs so that the resulting organs will more closely resemble those found in humans and thus be less likely to be rejected.

Cloning

Work on transgenic animals has also led to the cloning of entire organisms. A clone is an identical genetic copy of an organism—its DNA is the same as that of the original from which the copy was made. In humans, identical twins are naturally occurring clones. In these cases, the original fertilized egg divides into two genetically identical halves and proceeds to develop into two distinct babies. Since the babies originated from the same egg fertilized by the same sperm, they have exactly the same DNA. By contrast, fraternal twins come from two separate eggs, each of which is fertilized by a different sperm cell. Even though these children are born at the same time, they are as genetically different from each other as any other pair of siblings born years apart would be.

The cloning of organisms must be carefully distinguished from the cloning of genes—a distinction that the popular media have not always succeeded in making. The cloning of single genes, using plasmids, is an established procedure; the cloning of organisms is still experimental and highly controversial. Although several fringe groups claim to have successfully cloned human beings, they have failed—as of the writing of this book—to produce any evidence to support their contentions.

To this date, the most famous cloned mammal remains Dolly the sheep. A close look at how Dolly was created will provide a good description of the techniques required to clone any higher animal, including humans. In announcing Dolly's birth in 1997, *Scientific American* magazine reported:

> Dolly, unlike any other mammal that has ever lived, is an identical copy of another adult and has no father. She is a clone, the creation of a group of veterinary researchers. That work, performed by Ian Wilmut and his colleagues at the Roslin Institute in Edinburgh, Scotland, has provided an important new research tool and has shattered a belief widespread among biologists that cells from adult mammals cannot be persuaded to regenerate a whole animal.[21]

Previously, researchers had cloned mammals and other animals using embryonic cells as a starting point. Embryonic cells, taken from an undeveloped fertilized egg, are different from adult cells in that they are undifferentiated. When an egg cell is fertilized, it starts to divide. Up to a certain point, the cells in each succeeding generation have the ability to develop into specialized cells that will make up the various parts (organs, bones, skin, etc.) of the mature organism. After that point, cells become differentiated, or specialized—some of them begin to turn into liver cells, others into brain cells, and so on. Until Dolly, it was thought that clones could be produced only from undifferentiated cells that would divide and grow to maturity as the cloned organism developed.

Promise and Problems of Cloning

Dolly, however, was cloned from a cell taken from the udder of a six-year-old female sheep, a fully developed adult. Dolly was the 277th attempt made by Wilmut and his fellow researchers. The other attempts had

Scotland's Dolly the sheep was the world's first cloned mammal.

failed, but the same technique was used in all of them. "Wilmut and his co-workers accomplished their feat by transferring the nuclei from various types of sheep cells into unfertilized sheep eggs from which the natural nuclei had been removed by micro-surgery," the *Scientific American* article continues.

> Once the transfer was complete, the recipient eggs contained a complete set of genes, just as they would do if they had been fertilized by sperm. The eggs were then cultured for a period before being implanted into sheep that carried them to term, one of which culminated in a successful birth. The resulting lamb was, as expected, an exact genetic copy, or clone, of the sheep that provided the transferred nucleus, not of [the sheep] that pro-vided the egg.[22]

Wilmut used a pipette many times thinner than a human hair to remove the DNA from the host egg. Then the empty egg was placed next to a cell taken from the donor sheep's udder and the two were fused together using a tiny jolt of electricity. Another pulse of electricity caused the egg cell, with its new DNA, to start dividing. The cell was now behaving just like a normal egg cell would if it had been fertil-ized by sperm from a male sheep. It was cultured for a few days in a laboratory dish and then implanted into the uterus of a third sheep, which carried it to term and gave birth to Dolly.

From the beginning, Wilmut and other geneticists were concerned that since Dolly's DNA came from a six-year-old sheep she might age prematurely. At first, she seemed to be perfectly healthy and gave birth to a lamb of her own in 1998. But then Dolly began to develop medical problems frequently associ-ated with aging. "Early in life Dolly had a weight problem. Then in 1999, it emerged that caps at her chromosome ends called telomeres, which get shorter each time a cell divides, were 20 percent shorter than

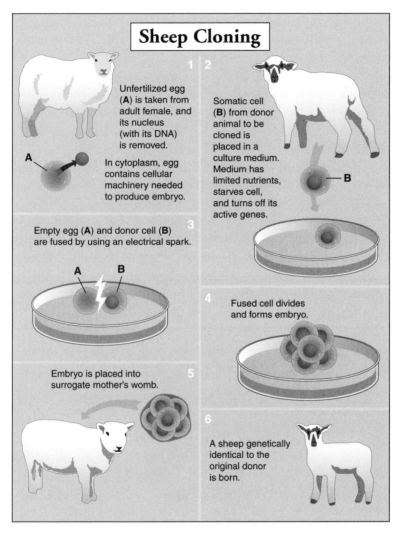

Sheep Cloning

1. Unfertilized egg (**A**) is taken from adult female, and its nucleus (with its DNA) is removed.

   In cytoplasm, egg contains cellular machinery needed to produce embryo.

2. Somatic cell (**B**) from donor animal to be cloned is placed in a culture medium. Medium has limited nutrients, starves cell, and turns off its active genes.

3. Empty egg (**A**) and donor cell (**B**) are fused by using an electrical spark.

4. Fused cell divides and forms embryo.

5. Embryo is placed into surrogate mother's womb.

6. A sheep genetically identical to the original donor is born.

was normal for a sheep her age," says science journalist John Whitfield, writing in the journal *Nature*. "This led to speculation that Dolly's biological age might equal that of her and her mother combined."[23]

In 2002, Dolly was diagnosed with arthritis, another disease associated with old age, and then she came down with lung cancer. Dolly was humanely put to death at the age of six and a half years, half the normal life span of a sheep of her kind. Cloned animals since Dolly, including cows, rabbits, mice, cats, goats, and pigs, have experienced similar problems. "Dolly's premature death is typical of cloned animals," Whitfield writes.

> From conception onwards, clones suffer a higher mortality rate than non-clones. Studies in mice seem to show that this bad health persists throughout life. Some seized upon Dolly's ailments as evidence that clones are invariably sickly and age prematurely. Although it can't be ruled out that her origins made her less robust than other sheep, it is not possible to make generalizations about clones' health from the fate of a single animal. . . . But the process of genetic reprogramming seems too complex and haphazard to control tightly, and its success rate has not improved much since Dolly's day.[24]

Genetically engineering oversized cattle to increase beef yield is just one of the potential benefits of cloning.

Although many questions about animal cloning remain to be answered, scientists are hopeful that, as

with genetically engineered plants, there are many benefits in store. Among these are creating oversized cattle to improve beef yield and the production of stem cells, multipurpose cells found in embryos, which may prove to have a wide range of medical applications. Like transgenic plants, transgenic animals can be created to produce greater amounts of nutrients, and some scientists also claim that cloning can be used to preserve endangered species from extinction.

The Human Genome Project

The human genome is composed of about 3 billion base pairs of As and Ts, Gs and Cs. In 1990, an international consortium of scientists set out to create a map that would show exactly where on our twenty-three pairs of chromosomes every one of those base pairs is located. The effort, called the Human Genome Project, is the most extensive scientific enterprise ever undertaken.

Genetic mapping is the first step in isolating a gene. There are two basic approaches to this complex endeavor. The first is called linkage mapping, and its goal is to show where on each chromosome each gene is located relative to other genes. The method is to compare the genetic makeup of members of a family or closely related group of people who have a history of a specific disease. By finding similar base pairs on the chromosomes of family members in succeeding generations of this group who have the disease, scientists can isolate the responsible gene and begin to build a map of the entire genome. The second type of map is far more ambitious. It is called a physical map and its goal is to show the absolute (not relative) location of the base pairs that make up every gene.

In both cases, the cut-and-paste techniques developed by genetic engineering are indispensable. Restriction enzymes are used to cut the chromosomes into small segments, which are then cut into even smaller pieces until the sought-after gene is found. It is a painstaking process, made possible not only by the methods of genetic engineering, but also by powerful supercomputers that enable researchers to compare various overlapping segments to weed out duplicate base pairs and base pairs that appear not to play any role in the process of genetic inheritance. Only about 2 percent of the 3 billion base pairs actually make up functional genes. The rest, called junk DNA, help to locate the genes and may play other roles that remain to be determined.

The Human Genome Project was virtually completed in the year 2003. It yielded many interesting—and surprising—insights into the genetic composition of human beings. Among them: the total number of genes in a human being lies between 30,000 and 35,000, far fewer than earlier estimates of 80,000 to 140,000; the average gene consists of about 3,000 base pairs, but sizes vary greatly, the longest being 2.4 million base pairs; 99.9 percent of base pairs are identical in all people; the function of more than 50 percent of human genes has not yet been determined. While work continues on tracking down the roles played by these mystery genes, the next step is the mapping of the human proteome—the complete array of proteins operating in the human body. This includes pinpointing all the proteins coded for by the genes and describing the specific role these proteins play in the human organism.

Chapter 4

Genes and Health

The discoveries of twentieth-century genetics in general, and the Human Genome Project in particular, have launched medicine on a whole new course. Rather than waiting for diseases to develop and then treating them with drugs or surgery, doctors are now embarked on finding the genetic causes of disease in the hope of fixing the malfunctioning gene before the illness even begins to show its early symptoms. In addition to repairing faulty genes, medical researchers now have within their grasp the ability to analyze individual genomes—the total genetic makeup of specific organisms—to see if they have a full complement of genes and to add healthy versions of those that are missing.

Mutation

Not all ailments are genetic diseases, but it is becoming increasingly apparent that genes play some role in almost everything that can go wrong with a human being. Defects in genes, or genes that fail to appear altogether, are due to a process called mutation. The concept of mutation covers a wide range of circumstances. "Mutations are alterations in existing genes," says evolutionary biologist Dennis O'Neil. "They can be as small as a point mutation, which is a change in a single DNA condon [three base pairs in a DNA sequence that specify the instructions for making an amino acid] or as large as a major structural modification in chromosomes and even missing or extra chromosomes."[25]

Mutations are very common, and not all are debilitating to the carrier. "In order for a mutation to be inherited, it must occur in the genetic material of a sex cell," O'Neil says.

Estimates of the frequency of mutations in human sex cells generally are about one per 10 to 100,000 for any specific gene. Since humans have approximately 32,000 genes, it is to be expected that most sex cells contain at least one mutation of some sort. In other words, mutations are probably common occurrences even in healthy people. Most mutations probably do not confer a significant advantage or disadvantage. They are relatively neutral in their effect. However, some are extremely serious and result in death before birth, when an individual is still in the embryonic or early stages of fetal development.[26]

If a mutation occurs in a somatic cell, it will affect only that person in whose body the cell resides. If, however, it occurs in a sex cell—sperm or egg—it will be passed on to the next generation, as O'Neil points out. Mutations occur when DNA replicates itself. The process is extremely complex. The long, twisted DNA molecule straightens out and splits down the center. Each nucleotide (each A, C, T, and G) is separated from its original partner. As the process of replication continues, each of these nucleotide letters gets paired up with a new partner, an A with a T, a C with a G. In order for this to happen, many individual biochemical reactions have to take place. One little slip, and a mutation occurs.

Cells have a way of checking to make sure that replication takes place as it is supposed to, but because thousands of base pairs are involved for each gene, the mechanism occasionally fails. In those cases, a gene is created that does not contain the correct information to produce the proteins that it nor-

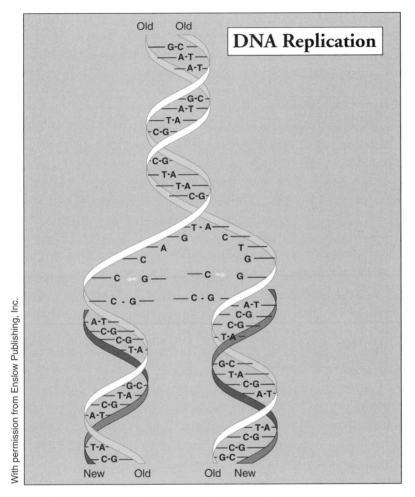

mally makes. Since proteins produce an organism's traits, a trait will be affected whenever a replication failure happens. Some of these miscues are relatively harmless, but others can lead to the catastrophes we refer to as genetic diseases.

One way to conceptualize this process is to think of the gene as a recipe for an amino acid (amino acids are the building blocks of proteins). Each line of the recipe is a sequence of As, Ts, Cs, and Gs. If a mutation occurs, the letters get out of order and the recipe produces an amino acid other than the intended one. When that amino acid combines with others, either a different protein will result or, in some mismatches, no protein at all will be produced. Depending on the role that protein plays in the functioning of the body, the end of the process may be a disease, perhaps a deadly one.

Genetic Disease

So far, medical scientists have identified almost ten thousand diseases stemming from genetic mutation. As researchers study the information gleaned from the Human Genome Project further, more genetic disease will be discovered. But it is important to realize that not all mutations are bad. In fact, mutations have made evolution possible. "The great diversity of life forms that have been identified in the fossil record is evidence that there has been an accumulation of mutations producing a more or less constant supply of both small and large variations upon which natural selection has operated for billions of years," O'Neil says. "Mutation has been the essential prerequisite for the evolution of life."[27]

Scientists cannot yet identify the specific causes of genetic mutation. It is suspected that environmental factors may play a role in some instances of this phenomenon, but most mutations are thought to occur spontaneously. In other words, they happen by chance and there is no way to control them, given the complexity of DNA replication. But, although they cannot be controlled, their effects can be studied because they take the form, most commonly, of abnormalities in the characteristics that make up the organism in which they occur. By tracing the abnormality backward to the cause using genetic linkage maps, scientists have been able to relate certain disease to certain mutations. This is the scientific basis for genetic medicine.

It has become apparent that large genes, simply because they are made up of many base pairs, are more susceptible to mutation than small genes and that most genetic diseases are caused by defects in more than one gene. However, many genetic diseases are the result of a single point mutation (a single-letter misspelling in the genetic code) in a single gene. Sickle-cell anemia, a blood disorder that affects mostly people of African descent, is one such disease. It is so typical of this type of genetic disease that a brief description will provide a good basis for understanding this phenomenon.

Sickle-Cell Anemia

Sickle-cell anemia is not contagious; no one can catch it from another person. The only way to contract the disease is to inherit it from one's parents. It manifests itself as a defect in the shape of red blood cells that interferes with their ability to transport oxygen to other cells in the body. Normal red blood

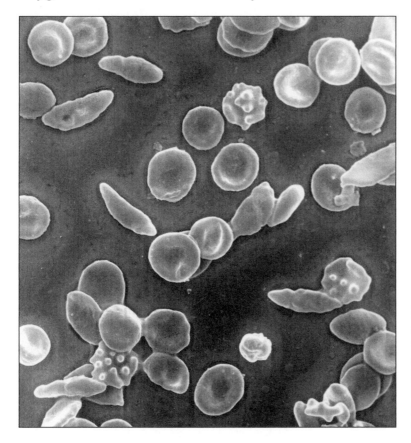

Elongated red blood cells, pictured here with normal, doughnut-shaped red blood cells, are characteristic of the genetic disease sickle-cell anemia.

cells are doughnut-shaped. In persons suffering from sickle-cell anemia, the cells are shaped like a half-moon or sickle, hence the disease's name. These sickle-shaped cells are unstable and break apart easily, clogging or damaging blood vessels, leading to pain, lung damage, and, in some cases, heart and brain damage as well.

Sickle-cell anemia is a recessive genetic disease, meaning that to contract it, a child must inherit two defective alleles of the relevant gene, one from each parent. In this way, it is similar to the shortness trait that Gregor Mendel noticed in his pea plants. Recessiveness is one reason why sickle-cell anemia is so insidious. People with only one allele for the disease will show no symptoms and therefore may be unaware that they are carrying the defective gene. It is only when two affected people produce offspring together that sickle-cell anemia occurs.

Sickle-cell anemia was first described in medical literature in 1910, but it was not until 1948 that Nobel Prize–winner Linus Pauling discovered that the hemoglobin, a protein in red blood cells, in people with sickle-cell anemia was different from that in nonsufferers, making sickle-cell anemia the first disease in which an abnormal protein was known to be at fault. Then, in 1956, two British medical researchers, Vernon Ingram and J.A. Hunt, carried out an experiment to sequence the hemoglobin from the blood of a person with sickle cell. They found that an expected amino acid had been replaced by another. Knowing which sequences of As, Ts, Cs, and Gs coded for both proteins, they were able to work backward and discover the genetic mutation responsible. That made sickle-cell anemia the first genetic disorder for which an adequate molecular explanation was known.

"People who inherit two genes for sickle hemoglobin (one from each parent) have sickle cell disease," says Dr. Kenneth R. Bridges.

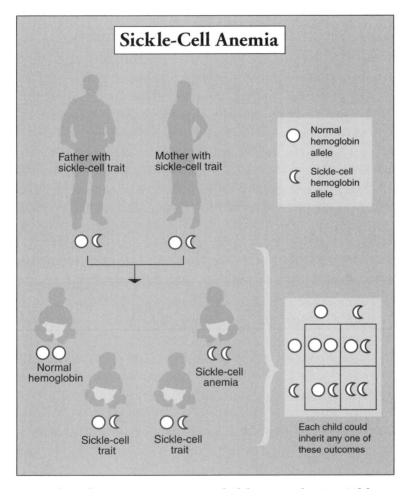

Sickle-Cell Anemia

Father with sickle-cell trait

Mother with sickle-cell trait

○ Normal hemoglobin allele

☾ Sickle-cell hemoglobin allele

Normal hemoglobin

Sickle-cell anemia

Sickle-cell trait

Sickle-cell trait

Each child could inherit any one of these outcomes

With a few exceptions, a child can inherit sickle cell disease only if both parents have one gene for sickle cell hemoglobin. . . . [Following Gregor Mendel's ratios for recessive inheritance] a one-in-four chance exists that a child will inherit two normal genes from the parents. A one-in-four chance also exists that a child will inherit two sickle cell genes, and have sickle cell disease. A one-in-two chance exists that the child will inherit a normal gene from one parent and a sickle gene from the other. This would produce the sickle trait.[28]

Thus, the basis for understanding genetic disease was laid down by Gregor Mendel when he studied inherited characteristics in garden peas. However, it took a century of work by molecular biologists to relate this discovery to the biochemical processes that govern it. Genetic medicine, and the great hope it has engendered, is the result. In the case of sickle-cell anemia, it is now possible to test prospective parents to see if either or both are carrying the sickle-cell trait, giving them the option of whether to have children who will be subject to the risk of inheriting the disease. "Newborns in most states are tested at birth by hemoglobin electrophoresis that detects sickle cell disease," Bridges says. "Newborn screening assures that children with sickle cell disease will receive proper care. In the past, some children died of complications of their sickle cell disease before the condition was diagnosed."[29]

It is now possible to fight sickle-cell anemia on two fronts, neither of which was possible before the advent of genetic medicine. Parents who are carrying the sickle-cell gene can choose not to pass it on to their children, and children who do have the disease can be treated with drug therapy early enough to avoid the most dire consequences of the condition, improving the quality and duration of their lives.

Gene Therapy

Progress has been made in identifying the cause of many other genetic diseases. These discoveries have not, in most cases, yielded a cure. However, further research may one day provide a cure or at least a test that will alert parents that they are likely to pass the defective genes on to their children and give them a chance not to.

Early detection of disease is just one of the ways in which genetics is transforming medicine. And it is one of the more primitive ways. With the completion of the Human Genome Project a whole new field has opened up. Instead of treating disease with

medications and/or surgery, scientists hope that genetic disorders can be corrected as soon as they are
identified by editing the letters—the As, Ts, Cs, and
Gs—that are responsible for the genetic abnormalities that cause the conditions. This field is called
gene therapy, and it involves repairing broken genes
or adding genes that are missing altogether from an
individual's genome.

Adenosine deaminase (ADA) deficiency is the first
disease combated with gene therapy. It is a cata-
strophic disorder of the immune system that always
results in death if it is not treated. "Gene therapy for
ADA was chosen for the first human gene therapy
for several reasons," says biologist Paul Heyman. "It
is the result of a mutation in one gene, making it
simple to replace. . . . Also, only a small amount of
ADA activity is needed for therapy to be effective,
while too much ADA does not seem to have a negative effect on humans."[30]

The first attempt to treat ADA deficiency with
gene therapy was carried out in 1990 by Dr. Michael
Blaese on two girls at the National Institutes of
Health Center for Human Genome Research in
Bethesda, Maryland. Cells were removed from the
girls' blood, the deficient copies of the ADA gene
were removed using genetic engineering techniques,
and healthy versions of the genes were inserted in
their place. The genetically altered cells were cultured in a laboratory for several days and injected
into the girls' bloodstreams. The therapy continued
over two years, and the girls slowly began to show
signs of improvement. Today, their bodies produce
enough ADA to maintain their immune systems in a
satisfactory condition with the help of a supporting
drug.

A few years later, Blaese achieved even greater success in the treatment of ADA deficiency, using stem
cells—cells at an embryonic stage of development
before they differentiate into specialized cells that

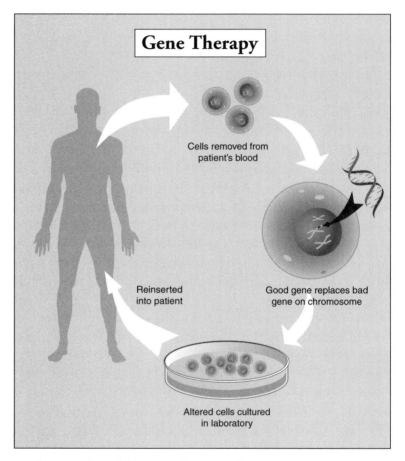

Gene Therapy

Cells removed from patient's blood

Good gene replaces bad gene on chromosome

Reinserted into patient

Altered cells cultured in laboratory

make up the different kinds of tissue that compose the human body. Blaese and his colleagues "identified three fetuses with inherited abnormal ADA genes," Heyman says. "Upon delivery of the babies, the researchers obtained stem cells from the blood in the umbilical cords of the babies and inserted functional copies of the ADA gene. Four days after birth, the stem cells with the functional ADA gene were inserted into the three babies, who now have normal immune systems."[31] The difference between the two cases is that in the second, no additional drug therapy was needed to maintain the babies' immune systems in a healthy state.

Genetic therapy can also be employed to stop a gene from producing harmful proteins, rather than, as in the cases above, altering or adding a gene to produce a beneficial protein. This procedure is called antisense therapy. Doctors insert a modified gene that stops the defective gene from doing its negative work. Studies are also under way to create genetically engineered artificial chromosomes to combat diseases that are resistant to other forms of genetic treatment.

Ethical Problems

So far, gene therapy has been progressing at a very slow pace. Treatments are being tested for various types of cancer (especially those of the skin, head, and neck), cystic fibrosis, hemophilia, diabetes, Parkinson's disease, and certain forms of heart disease. Advances have been slowed by the difficulty of getting genetically modified genes into target cells and by the complexity of most genetic disease (unlike the two cases discussed above, most of these disorders are caused not by a single defective gene, but by several, thus multiplying the difficulty of designing an effective treatment).

Ethical considerations have also put a brake on research. In 1998, eighteen-year-old Jesse Gelsinger, who was suffering from a liver ailment called ornithine transcarbolzylase deficiency, volunteered to test an experimental gene therapy at the University of Pennsylvania. Soon after modified genes were introduced into his body by means of a virus related to the virus that causes the common cold, his immune system went into overdrive. First, it attacked the virus, then his liver, kidneys, lungs, and brain. Four days later he was dead. The federal government immediately tightened restrictions on human testing of gene therapies, resulting in the cancellation of many promising research projects. Gelsinger's death started an international debate on the ethics of genetic research on humans, and most experts expressed the opinion that more restraint was needed.

Many scientists believe that stem cells like these could be used to grow organs for transplants. Ethical concerns, however, have slowed the progress of stem cell research.

Other ethical issues have also held up the application of advances in genetic engineering to medical practice. Stem cells, taken from human embryos before they develop into specialized cells, may someday allow scientists to grow whole replacement organs for transplant purposes. But the most fruitful source of stem cells is embryos that are destroyed when the stem cells are harvested, thus putting this entire area of research into the middle of the abortion debate, one of the most divisive social issues of recent years. The federal administration has chosen to withhold funding for experimental stem cell programs unless researchers agree to use only stem cells cloned from a relatively few already-existing strains. Many scientists question the quality of these cells and maintain that the restrictions will drastically limit advances in this area.

Despite these disappointments, genetic research pioneer W. French Anderson believes that gene ther-

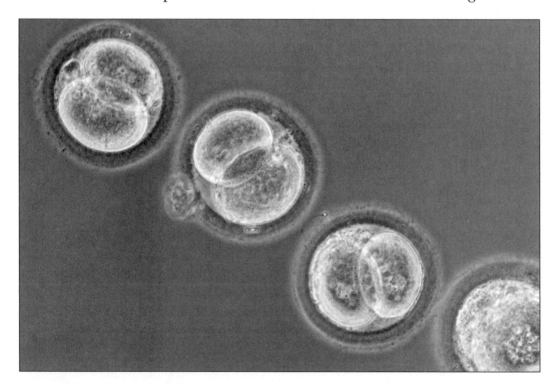

apy will play a crucial role in the future of medicine. "The field of gene therapy has been criticized for promising too much and providing too little," he says.

> But gene therapy, like every other major new technology, takes time to develop. Antibiotics, monoclonal antibodies, organ transplants, to name just a few areas of medicine, have taken many years to mature. Major new technologies in every field, such as the manned rocket to the moon, had failures and disappointments. Early hopes are always frustrated by the many incremental steps necessary to produce "success." Gene therapy will succeed with time. And it is important that it does succeed, because no other area of medicine holds as much promise for providing cures for the many devastating diseases that now ravage humankind.[32]

Chapter 5

Genes and the Law

Besides blazing new paths in health science, genetics is transforming the way in which criminal investigations and trials are conducted. The importance of DNA evidence rests on a single but crucial fact: Every individual's DNA is unique (except in the case of identical twins, who have identical genomes). A person's DNA profile can be used like a fingerprint to link suspects to crime scenes and victims. DNA profiling—also called DNA fingerprinting or DNA typing—has been responsible for overturning verdicts and saving innocent people from execution. The process is complicated and controversial. Nevertheless, it has earned itself a place in police probes and courtroom proceedings, and the science behind it is compelling enough that it is likely to play a major role in the future.

The Battle over DNA

Proponents of DNA analysis had to fight against strenuous opposition before the judicial system consented to recognize its validity in courtroom proceedings. "In its early days, DNA was highly controversial and not always accepted by the courts," says James F. Crow of the Genetics Department at the University of Wisconsin in Madison:

The arguments and uncertainties led to a study by the National Academy of Sciences. Publication of this report started with a bang. A badly mangled report by the usually reliable *New York Times* implied that there should be a moratorium on DNA use. This was followed the next day by a front page retraction. The [National Academy of Sciences] report had made no such recommendation, although it raised a number of questions about the techniques and their interpretation.[33]

The NSF conducted further studies and concluded that DNA was, in fact, a valid tool in criminal investigation. "We strongly believe that DNA testing properly performed belongs in the courtroom," say Howard Coleman and Eric Swenson in a guide to the subject prepared for journalists.

We share this view with the U.S. Congress Office of Technology Assessment, the National Academy of Sciences and the vast majority of scientists in America. The continuing controversy over the admissibility of DNA evidence makes little sense except to the very few people who benefit from continued confusion.

The DNA war is a clash of the different approaches of law and science. It would be difficult to think of two disciplines that have more disparate approaches to seeking the truth. Scientific truth evolves by the building of consensus through peer review and the replicating of experiments. For the law, truth is less absolute and more relative to the case at hand. Legal truth is achieved through adversarial argument and judgment. The DNA war is a dramatic, hard-fought conflict between these two worlds.[34]

DNA evidence can be gathered from a wide variety of sources, including blood, semen, hair, fingernails and toenails, saliva, urine, skin, and other body tissues. The DNA of every human being is 99.9 percent

DNA evidence can be gathered by taking samples of a person's saliva, hair, or fingernails.

similar to that of every other human being; however, since there are more than 3 billion base pairs to consider, that 0.1 percent difference is equivalent to 3 million ways in which each genome can be uniquely different. These differences manifest themselves as different arrangements of As, Ts, Cs, and Gs, called DNA polymorphisms. These lie in vast stretches of DNA known as noncoding, DNA, or the DNA that lies between genes on each chromosome.

Noncoding DNA, or junk DNA as it is also called, is characterized by sequences of letters (As, Ts, Cs, and Gs) that repeat in a regular manner up to thirty times in a row. These patterns are called variable number tandem repeats (VNTRs), and it is extremely unlikely that any two individuals will have similar patterns of repeating junk DNA provided that a sufficiently large number of patterns are observed. The key circumstance in DNA evidence is that the number of VNTRs at specific locations on the chromosomes differs between individuals. The fundamental technique used to determine a DNA profile is called restriction fragment length polymorphisms (RFLPs). This complicated phrase simply means that investigators determine the number of VNTR repeats at a series of distractive locations in order to come up with an individual's profile. An alternative method is to use a polymerase chain reaction (PCR). RFLP testing requires more DNA, from 20 to 50 billionths of a gram, to be accurate. PCR requires only 2 billionths of a gram.

DNA Profiles

To create a DNA profile, the following steps must be followed. First, DNA is taken from the crime scene. The DNA can come from any body fluid or tissue left behind. The DNA must be cleaned up to make sure that it has not been contaminated by dust, soil, carpet fibers, or other extraneous substances. Every cell will contain a complete copy of the subject's entire genome, far too much genetic material to be analyzed all at once. Therefore, the DNA is cut into manageable pieces using restriction enzymes that were developed as part of the tool kit of genetic engineering. The choice of which restriction enzymes to use is important. They should not cut the DNA within the VNTR locations that are being examined. Ideally, they should do their work just outside a VNTR region.

Once the DNA has been reduced to fragments, the pieces, which range in size from one hundred to ten thousand base pairs, are sorted according to length. The process used to do this is called gel electrophoresis. The DNA fragments are placed on a flat tray in a chemical gel called agarose. The tray is then placed in an electric field. Since the DNA has a negative charge, it will be pulled toward the positive electrode, and larger pieces will progress more slowly than smaller ones. The relative size of each fragment of DNA is determined by how far it has moved through the agarose in a given period of time.

To prevent the fragments of DNA from decomposing, they are uncoiled from their spiral (double helix) form and affixed to a nylon membrane that has been treated with preservatives. The DNA pieces are then attached to radioactive probes that identify each VNTR location. The radioactive probe can be photographed on X-ray film to provide a visual image of the microscopic letters in the VNTR sequence. These show up on the film as a series of dark bands that appear similar to the bar codes on consumer items. To obtain a complete genetic profile, this procedure has to be repeated for a number of VNTR locations on different chromosomes. If the profile is based on thirteen different locations, the standard used by the Federal Bureau of Investigation (FBI) and many other law enforcement organizations, the chances that the DNA sample can be linked to the wrong individual are approximately one in 100 billion.

However, crime scenes can be very messy places. DNA from the victim, or victims if there are more than one, frequently gets mixed with that of the suspect or suspects. The precision of DNA profiling is often complicated by these and other circumstances. "The interpretation of the data . . . requires that inferences based on the science of statistics, population genetics and probability theory be applied to

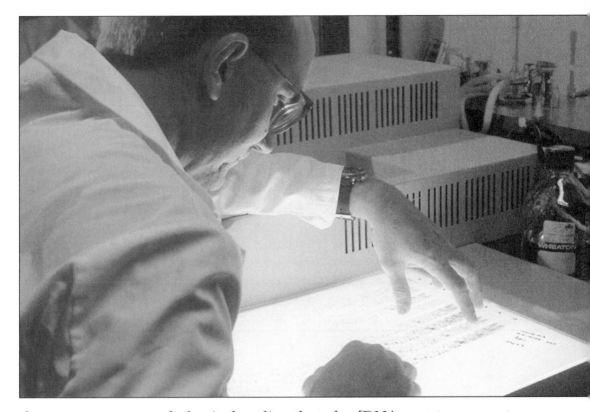

the measurements of physical reality that the [DNA tests] reveal," say Coleman and Swenson. "Forensic scientists use these mathematical concepts to calculate and report an estimate of how frequently the genetic profile they have observed might be found in major population groups."[35]

A laboratory worker studies a DNA profile. DNA testing has been a vital tool in criminal investigations since it was first used in 1987.

DNA's Courtroom Debut

DNA evidence was first used in a courtroom in the mid-1980s. In one early case, it was employed to exonerate one suspect and convict another. Police in the East Midlands area of England were struggling to solve the brutal rape and murder of two schoolgirls. Their prime suspect was a kitchen worker at a nearby mental hospital. The police brought samples of the worker's blood and samples of semen taken from the crime scenes to geneticist Alec Jeffreys at the University of Leicester for analysis. Jeffreys was able to conclude that the same person had committed both crimes, but that the perpetrator was not the kitchen worker.

Police were convinced that the killer was a local resident, so they requested that every male in town between the ages of seventeen and thirty-four submit a blood sample for testing. Within a few months more than 4,583 DNA tests had been performed and none of them matched the DNA retrieved from the crime scene semen. The authorities were about to fall back on more conventional investigative methods when they were informed by a bakery manager that one of her employees, a man named Colin Pitchfork, had persuaded a coworker to be tested in his place. When officers confronted Pitchfork, he confessed to the rapes and murders. When the police lab tested his DNA, they found it matched perfectly the samples taken from the sites where the two girls were killed.

The date was September 1987, and DNA testing has been a vital tool in criminal investigations ever since. DNA testing spread from England to America, where it quickly became a major weapon in the war against crime. The mass media hailed it as a virtually infallible way to determine guilt or innocence. Even judges were overwhelmed by its apparent ability to cut through the often confusing and inconclusive nature of other forms of evidence. One judge, Joseph Harris, of Albany, New York, proclaimed that DNA evidence was the "greatest single advance in the search for truth since the advent of cross-examination."[36]

At first, defense attorneys were powerless to challenge the apparent certitude of DNA evidence. In more than a hundred cases, genetics played the decisive role in getting a conviction. Some legal experts felt that the phenomenon was eroding a defendant's right to a fair trial. "In rape cases, when the semen has been matched with the defendant's and the chance that it came from another person is 33 billion to one, you don't need a jury,"[37] complained lawyer Robert Bowser. But chinks soon began to appear in the seemingly invincible DNA armor—not because the science was faulty, but because the tests were extremely complicated and the laboratories where they were conducted were prone to error.

DNA Challenged

The first case on which DNA evidence was successfully disputed took place in New York in 1987. A woman named Vilma Ponce, who was seven months pregnant, was found dead with more than sixty stab wounds on her body. Her two-year-old daughter lay murdered in a similarly brutal way in the bathroom of Ponce's apartment. The principal suspect was José Castro, a janitor in a nearby apartment building. Detectives found a blood stain on his watch. DNA tests conducted by an independent laboratory indicated that the blood on Castro's watch matched Ponce's blood. The odds against the blood being from someone else were put at one in 189 million.

Castro's defense lawyer challenged the test results and produced witnesses who testified that the lab had not followed accepted procedures. The DNA evidence was thrown out of court and Castro appeared to be on his way to acquittal when he suddenly confessed to the crime. The DNA evidence was correct, but it was not allowed to be presented to the jury because the laboratory's procedures for handling such evidence were deemed to be too lax.

The scientific basis of applying genetics to criminal proceedings has never been questioned; what has neutralized much such evidence has been sloppiness on the part of lab technicians and police investigators in handling the samples upon which the DNA tests were conducted. The most famous trial in which DNA evidence played a role was that of former football star O.J. Simpson, who was accused in 1994 of murdering his ex-wife, Nicole Brown Simpson, and her friend Ron Goldman. The prosecution produced DNA evidence that appeared overwhelmingly to link Simpson to the crime scene. Yet the jury refused to convict him. His defense attorneys did not challenge the validity of DNA testing in general. In fact, they distanced themselves from the laboratory procedures that were done. What they did attack—successfully—was how police investigators handled the blood samples once they had been collected. By focusing on breaks in the chain of evidence, how samples were passed from one investigator to another, how long and under what circumstances they were stored, and a number of other irregularities, the defense team managed to convince the jury that the possibility existed that the samples had been tampered with. It was enough to create "reasonable doubt" as to Simpson's guilt in the minds of the jurors and led to his acquittal. Again, the scientific basis of DNA analysis was never in question, but science alone was not the deciding factor in the outcome of the trial.

A forensic scientist places blood samples into evidence envelopes. Careless handling of samples and other lab mistakes can make DNA data unusable in court.

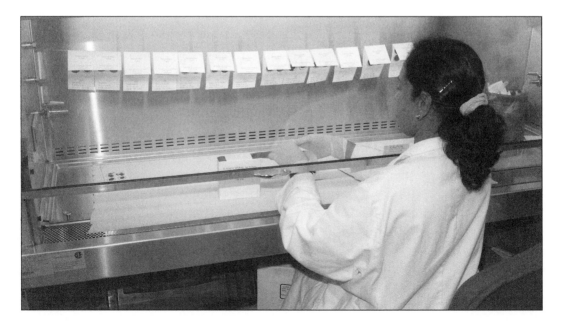

Paternity Testing

Determining guilt or innocence in criminal investigations is not the only application of DNA technology to legal matters. The technique is used even more frequently in paternity testing, with approximately two hundred thousand such tests being performed every year. It has all but supplanted conventional blood tests as a convenient, accurate way to determine the identity of a child's father. While blood tests can conclusively prove that a man is not the father of a child, they cannot determine beyond doubt that he is.

DNA tests, on the other hand, provide almost 100 percent assurance in either case. Moreover, blood tests must be performed by licensed doctors, whereas DNA tests can be done by a wide range of qualified technicians. In many cases, all that is required is a cotton swab rubbed on the inside of the cheek. In addition, blood tests could not be performed on babies until they were six months old. DNA samples can be taken immediately after birth—or while the baby is still in the womb. Finally, DNA can be obtained from the remains of a deceased father to establish whether or not a child is entitled to a share of his estate.

Paternity testing is possible because every individual contains two copies, or alleles, of every gene, one from the mother and the other from the father. If a child has an allele that did not come from the mother, then it must have come from the biological father. Conversely, if the allele in question is shown not to have come from the suspected father, paternity is disproved.

"Most paternity testing is done for financial reasons, i.e. to establish legal responsibility and provide for child support," say Coleman and Swenson.

> Even more important are the emotional and social issues. When testing can demonstrate conclusively

to a man that he is the father of a child, then he is more likely to provide not only financial support, but emotional support as well. He may bond with the child and take an active part in its life. . . . It wasn't very long ago that obtaining a paternity test was an uncertain, expensive and inconvenient process. . . . DNA testing has made the process convenient and the result conclusive. In all but the rarest of instances, the DNA test results provide a level of certainty so high that paternity will, for all practical purposes, be proven or disproved.[38]

Streamlining the Justice System

DNA paternity tests can also be used to prove childhood sexual abuse. Often in these cases, the allegation is not made until years after the event, when physical evidence that a crime has taken place is no longer available. If the abuse resulted in pregnancy, the tests can easily and definitively determine paternity and hence identify the perpetrator.

Barry Scheck, one of O.J. Simpson's defense attorneys, is the cofounder of the Innocence Project, an organization that has been fighting to get false convictions overturned on the basis of DNA evidence. He believes that genetic testing will streamline the criminal justice system by enabling police to determine at a preliminary stage whether a suspect was at the scene of the crime independently of often unreliable eyewitness testimony. "One of the things that we have to recognize about DNA testing is that we can use it . . . in an earlier stage of the investigation than it is being used today," Scheck says. "We can take smaller amounts of sample and test them at the beginning of the investigation. . . . We can now use DNA to get suspects and to eliminate the wrong people very, very early in the investigation."[39]

Scheck insists that the key to the success of DNA testing in the courts is the proper handling of samples by the police and by the laboratories where the tests are carried out. "DNA testing is truly revolutionary," he says. "It's transforming the way we do business in the criminal justice system. And it's only beginning. That's one reason why it's very important to make sure that the testing itself is done correctly, is done with the highest standards of quality assurance so that we don't make mistakes."[40]

Scheck believes that DNA testing will be able to exonerate many innocent people who are now in prison after having been falsely convicted on the basis of other types of evidence. It can also shed light on troubling, unsolved cases and prevent further crime by getting dangerous individuals off the streets. "We can go back to these old cases and see whether or not the system made mistakes," he says. "We can look at old, unsolved cases and find the real perpetrator."[41]

Finally, DNA testing, because it is relatively cheap, can help accused people with few resources at their disposal mount an effective defense. Scheck cites the Simpson case, in which, despite the Hall-of-Fame football player's wealth and the top-quality lawyers it enabled him to hire, the prosecution still had a preponderance of resources on its side. "The prosecution had 47 prosecutors working on the case. FBI, Interpol, the Los Angeles Police Department, the crime lab had tremendous resources, much greater than ours, but the point was . . . we were able to demonstrate that a lot of things went wrong."[42]

Genetics and the Definition of "Human"

The genetic revolution holds out great promise in medicine and many other fields. At the beginning of the twenty-first century, rapid advances in this relatively new science have put within humanity's grasp the ability to cure or prevent previously incurable diseases. The hope also exists of ending world hunger through the use of high-yield bioengineered food crops. But, despite all the positive aspects, genetic engineering raises some troubling questions that both experts and laymen will have to confront in the years immediately ahead. One of these questions may even entail a radical redefinition of what it means to be a human being, challenging some of our most deeply held philosophical and religious beliefs.

Designer Babies

Few people would dispute the benefits of a genetic procedure that could replace a gene that causes a horrific disease with a healthy version of the gene, even if the replacement was done on a fetus. It would spare the child great suffering and provide the chance to lead a normal life. But that same procedure could be used to enhance traits that are not classified as diseases. Parents could choose, for example, to give their unborn child blond hair rather than brown, blue eyes rather than green. They could opt to introduce or modify genes that would make the child taller and more muscular than the genes the child inherited naturally. The parents could also be tempted to alter genes to make the child more intelligent and more aggressive, and hence more likely to succeed in life.

A poll conducted by *Time* magazine reveals that 46 percent of parents in America would chose favorable traits for their children if the opportunity was available. Of those, 33 percent said intelligence would be the trait they would be most interested in enhancing; 11 percent said they would like the chance to choose the sex of their baby. Alarmingly, in another

Advances in genetic engineering may someday allow parents to select the sex, eye color, or intelligence level of their children. This possibility raises serious ethical concerns for many people.

poll, almost half the people interviewed said they would choose to abort a fetus if genetic tests showed that it was likely to grow up to be obese. These possibilities raise a number of troubling ethical concerns that humanity will have to grapple with as the techniques of genetic engineering are perfected in the decades to come. The phenomenon, popularly labeled designer babies, has far-reaching implications for our understanding of what it is to be a human being and for what kind of society we will create for future generations.

The debate must take into account the fact of economic disparity. The new genetic technologies will be expensive, so only the rich will be able to afford them. Science writer Colin Tudge says:

> Human beings in the future will practice cloning and will manipulate the genomes of their offspring to the point where they will, in effect, produce a new stratum of society. These will be the "Genrich" people, as opposed to the rest of us who are content (or stuck) with the genes we inherited by normal means. . . . The Genrich might eventually evolve into a new species: able to mate successfully with each other but not with the [genetically] unmanipulated.[43]

Of course, it is not now possible to manipulate genes on the intricate level that Tudge envisions. Intelligence, for example, is believed to result from the interaction of more than a hundred different genes and the further interaction of that genetic makeup with the environment in which a child is raised. But experts are virtually unanimous that the complexities will someday be overcome—perhaps before the end of the current century.

Eugenics

It is not the first time that human beings have tried to alter human nature. Just as farmers have attempted since the beginning of civilization to produce better livestock through selective breeding, there have at times erupted social movements to improve the human race through a process called eugenics. The term *eugenics* was coined in the nineteenth century, based on ancient Greek words that mean "well-born." This widespread social movement encouraged well-educated, affluent people to reproduce and discouraged those less privileged from doing so. The goal was to make the human race stronger, healthier, and more intelligent.

Eugenics presented its most gruesome face in Nazi Germany in the 1930s and 1940s, when the ruling party implemented policies to eradicate entire populations deemed to be undesirable, especially Jews, and to foster the growth of an ideal type of human being. But eugenics did not take root only in countries gripped by such a monstrous ideology; it found a welcoming home in Great Britain and the United States as well. By the early 1930s, thirty American states had enacted involuntary sterilization laws, designed to make it impossible for criminals and the mentally ill to reproduce. People with genetically transmittable diseases were also targeted.

With the stunning advances in genetic engineering, future eugenics programs would no longer be limited to the version of selective breeding advocated in the 1930s and 1940s. Now, science is on the verge of being able to test for desirable (and undesirable) traits using the much more far-reaching tools of genetic analysis. It is also on the point of being able to alter these traits while babies are still in the womb.

Who Gets to Choose?

Many observers are, understandably, troubled by the possibilities of a society controlled at the genetic level. The fear is that if the technology is available, it will be used by those who have access to it. This gives rise to two different sorts of problems. First, how can the public ever be sure that the manipulation of genes will be free from error? How can people guard against monstrous mistakes? What if, in an attempt to enhance the genes responsible for intelligence, scientists mistakenly create a whole new class of diseases? Such a tragic eventuality may not become apparent until the gene-altering procedure has been in use for decades. "In modern science as in ancient agriculture, the underlying theory, however coherent and satisfying, may not underpin the resulting technology as seems to be the case," Tudge says. "So the success of the resulting technology does not and cannot demonstrate that the underlying theory is correct and adequate in every respect. The theory must have been good enough to succeed in the particular case that was observed, but if the conditions were changed somewhat, inadequacies could well be revealed."[44]

Second, even if we do master the technology, which forces in society will determine who gets to benefit from it and who does not? The example of Nazi Germany makes most commentators reluctant to invest this authority in a political regime. But allowing the market forces of free enterprise to decide this important issue is, to some, equally unsatisfactory because those forces are biased in favor of the wealthy.

Without regulation, the poor tend to get left behind. Even if regulations were adopted to limit, or even ban altogether, the production of designer babies, people who wanted to profit by providing the technology and those wanting to benefit from it would find other options. Businesses involved in human cloning and the manipulation of the human genome could simply go underground or move to countries where regulations are not in force.

Human Nature

On a fundamental level, the genetic revolution has challenged the very notion of what it is to be a human being. Until the eruption of genetic engineering techniques in the late twentieth century, it was not possible to blend the genes of one species with those of another. When pigs mated, they gave birth to pigs; when humans mated they produced other human beings. Species lines have now become blurred.

It is possible to transplant pig genes into ailing humans to produce a protein in which the human was deficient. The technology promises to save lives and diminish suffering. But if a pig-to-human gene transposition is possible, so is the transfer of human genes into, say, our nearest genetic relative, the chimpanzee. Chimps are already highly intelligent creatures: Even without human intervention, they learn from each other and even have primitive cultures. What if a scientist transplanted the genes that

Scientists might one day be able to mix the genes of chimpanzees and other animals with those of humans. The result would be new species that are neither completely animal nor human.

give humans the ability to think abstractly and to communicate verbally into chimps? The resulting creature would be part human, but would it be human in the eyes of the law, for example?

Conversely, what if the genes that give cheetahs their speed and stamina were implanted into humans. The result would be a human-cheetah hybrid, a creature that was not fully a cheetah, but not fully a human either. Genetic engineering gives people the capacity to leap species barriers, with the consequence that the concept of humanity would have to change. "If we take the new technologies to their ultimate conclusion . . . then we will end up redesigning humanity," Tudge says. "Human beings, as we know them, will be superseded."[45]

Genetics is transforming the way in which people look at the world and at themselves. Never before have humans had the ability to intervene in the processes of life at such a basic level. The benefits, such as feeding the hungry and fighting disease, are obvious. The dangers—increased social inequality and maybe even the creation of a new species that will be stronger, smarter, healthier, and longer-lived than human beings—are equally apparent. The Age of Genetics is full of both promise and peril.

Notes

Introduction: The Age of Genetics

1. *Palm Beach Post*, "Genes: Who We Are, How We Age, What We Eat," April 12, 2002, p. 2A.

Chapter 1: Inheritance

2. Colin Tudge, *The Impact of the Gene: From Mendel's Peas to Designer Babies.* New York: Hill and Wang, 2000, pp. 8–9.
3. Tudge, *The Impact of the Gene*, p. 99.
4. R. Scott Hawley and Catherine A. Mori, *The Human Genome: A User's Guide.* San Diego: Academic Press, 1999, p. 13.
5. Hawley and Mori, *The Human Genome*, p. 13.
6. Hawley and Mori, *The Human Genome*, pp. 13–16.
7. Daniel L. Hartl and Elizabeth W. Jones, *Essential Genetics: A Genomics Perspective.* Sudbury, MA: Jones and Bartlett 2002, p. 40.

Chapter 2: Genes and DNA

8. William K. Purves et al., *"Life: The Science of Biology*, vol. 1, *The Cell and Heredity.* Salt Lake City: Sinauer, 1998, p. 76.
9. Laura Gould, *Cat's Are Not Peas: A Calico History of Genetics.* New York: Springer-Verlag, 1996, pp. 4–5.
10. Boyce Rensberger, *Life Itself: Exploring the Realm of the Living Cell.* New York: Oxford University Press, 1996, p. 88.
11. Rensberger, *Life Itself*, p. 90.
12. Hawley and Mori, *The Human Genome*, p. 19.
13. Paul Berg and Maxine Singer, *Dealing with Genes: The Language of Heredity.* Mill Valley, CA: University Science Books, 1992, p. 16.
14. Tudge, *The Impact of the Gene*, p. 126.

Chapter 3: Genetic Engineering

15. Karl Drlica, *Understanding DNA and Gene Cloning: A Guide for the Curious.* New York: John Wiley, 1997, p. 23.

16. Drlica, *Understanding DNA and Gene Cloning,* p. 123.
17. Maxim D. Frank-Kamenetskii, *Unraveling DNA: The Most Important Molecule of Life.* Reading, MA: Perseus Books, 1997, p. 55.
18. Frank-Kamenetskii, *Unraveling DNA,* p. 58.
19. Virginia Cooperative Extension, "Status Report on Transgenic Organisms." Charlottesville: University of Virginia, 1997, p. 2.
20. Electronic Forum on Biotechnology in Food and Agriculture, "How Appropriate Are Currently Available Biotechnologies in the Crop Sector for Food Production and Agriculture in Developing Countries." New York: Food and Agriculture Organization of the United Nations, 2000, p. 3.
21. Tim Beardsley, "A Clone in Sheep's Clothing," *Scientific American,* March 3, 2000. www.sciam.com.
22. Beardsley, "A Clone in Sheep's Clothing."
23. John Whitfield, "Obituary: Dolly the Sheep," *Nature,* February 19, 2003. www.nature.com.
24. Whitfield, "Obituary: Dolly the Sheep."

Chapter 4: Genes and Health

25. Dennis O'Neil "Mutation," Palomar College, 2002. http://anthro.palomar.edu.
26. O'Neil, "Mutation."
27. O'Neil, "Mutation."
28. Kenneth R. Bridges, "How Do People Get Sickle Cell Disease?" Harvard University, 2002. http://sickle.bwh. harvard.edu.
29. Bridges, "How Do People Get Sickle Cell Disease?"
30. Paul Heyman, Joanne Stark, and Ntobeko Ntusi, "ADA Deficiency," Haverford College, 1999. www.haverford.edu.
31. Heyman et al., "ADA Deficiency."
32. Quoted in Discovery Health Channel, "Cures." Discovery Communications, 2002. http:// health.discovery.com.

Chapter 5: Genes and the Law

33. James F. Crow, *DNA Forensics: Past, Present, and Future.* Madison, WI: Promega, 2000, p. 6.
34. Howard Coleman and Eric Swenson, *DNA in the Courtroom: A Trial Watcher's Guide.* Seattle: GeneLex Press, 1994. www. promega.com

35. Coleman and Swenson, *DNA in the Courtroom*, p. 31.
36. Quoted in Coleman and Swenson, *DNA in the Courtroom*, p. 10.
37. Quoted in Coleman and Swenson, *DNA in the Courtroom*, p. 10.
38. Coleman and Swenson, *DNA in the Courtroom*, p. 40.
39. Quoted in *Frontline*, "What Jennifer Saw." Public Broadcasting Service/WGBH, 1998. www.pbs.org.
40. Quoted in *Frontline*, "What Jennifer Saw."
41. Quoted in *Frontline*, "What Jennifer Saw."
42. Quoted in *Frontline*, "What Jennifer Saw."

Epilogue: Genetics and the Definition of "Human"
43. Tudge, *The Impact of the Gene*, p. 344.
44. Tudge, *The Impact of the Gene*, p. 315.
45. Tudge, *The Impact of the Gene*, p. 342.

Glossary

Adenosine deaminase (ADA) deficiency: Deficiency in the cells of an enzyme called adenosine deaminase, which plays a key role in the development of the immune system.

alleles: Alternate forms of a gene, inherited separately from each parent.

base pair: The pair of biochemicals that holds the strands of the DNA molecule together and provides a way to identify one gene from another.

chromosomes: The self-replicating genetic structures of cells containing the genes.

clone: A group of cells descended from a single ancestor cell.

cloning: The process by which a group of genetically identical cells are produced from a single ancestor cell.

DNA: The complex molecule that contains genetic information.

double helix: The shape of two intertwined strands of DNA.

gene: The fundamental unit of heredity.

gene expression: The process through which genes produce traits in organisms.

gene mapping: The method of determining the position of genes on chromosomes.

genome: The entire genetic material in the chromosomes of an organism.

human gene therapy: The introduction of DNA into cells to correct a genetic defect.

mutation: An inheritable change in the sequence of an organism's DNA.

Polymerase chain reaction (PCR): A quick and inexpensive technique for making copies of any fragment of DNA.

recombinant DNA technology: Another phrase for "genetic engineering," the procedures used to join fragments of DNA, either from a single organism or from multiple organisms.

Restriction fragment length polymorphisms (RFLPs): Variations in the length of DNA sequence fragments produced when genetic engineers cut DNA using a restriction enzyme.

Variable number tandem repeats (VNTRs): Repeating patterns of base pairs in a fragment of junk DNA.

For Further Reading

Books

Fran Balkwill, *DNA Is Here to Stay*. Minneapolis, MN: First Avenue Editions, 2003. This informatively illustrated account of the "molecule of life" brings the basics of genetics to life. The complexities of the subject are made simple by using pictures to amplify the carefully written text.

Norbert Landa and Patrick A. Baeuerie, *Ingenious Genes: Learning About the Fantastic Skills of Genetic Engineers and Watching Them at Work*. Hauppauge, NY: Barrons Juveniles, 1998. Landa and Baeuerie provide an ingenious look at how genetic scientists copy and change genes in the search for medical breakthroughs and other advances.

Cynthia Pratt Nicholson and Rose Cowles, *Baa! The Most Interesting Book You'll Ever Read About Genes and Cloning*. Tonawanda, NY: Kids Can Press, 2001. This brief survey covers a lot of material in relatively few words. It provides a lively account of genetics from Gregor Mendel to cloning, including a discussion of the ethical issues involved.

Websites

Human Genome Project Primers (www.orni.gov). This website is a gateway to the science underlying the Human Genome Project. It includes many links to stimulating discussions of the major issues involved.

Introduction to Genetics (www.emc.maricopa.edu). A well-illustrated and interactive discussion of the main points of genetics from a historical perspective.

Works Consulted

Books

Paul Berg and Maxine Singer, *Dealing with Genes: The Language of Heredity.* Mill Valley, CA: University Science Books, 1992. The authors try very hard to keep this book from becoming too technical for the average reader, but they do not always succeed. Basic information on genetics has to be extracted from discussions of more advanced topics.

Howard Coleman and Eric Swenson, *DNA in the Courtroom: A Trial Watcher's Guide.* Seattle: GeneLex Press, 1994. The authors provide a history of DNA forensics, an explanation of the science behind it, and a discussion of the controversies to which it has given rise.

Karl Drlica, *Understanding DNA and Gene Cloning: A Guide for the Curious.* New York: John Wiley, 1997. Drlica's goal is to explain the science behind the headlines appearing daily in newspapers around the world concerning the genetic revolution. He does so in easy-to-understand layman's terms.

Maxim D. Frank-Kamenetskii, *Unraveling DNA: The Most Important Molecule of Life.* Reading, MA: Perseus Books, 1997. This is a translation of a book that was originally published in Russia. The author discusses the history of DNA research and outlines future projects to be undertaken and problems to be overcome.

Laura Gould, *Cats Are Not Peas: A Calico History of Genetics.* New York: Springer-Verlag, 1996. Gould undertook the study of genetics to understand why her male calico cat was so rare. In an entertaining way, she covers all the basics of a complex science in simple language.

Daniel L. Hartl and Elizabeth W. Jones, *Essential Genetics: A Genomics Perspective.* Sudbury, MA: Jones and Bartlett, 2002.

This is a college-level introductory genetics textbook. It is up-to-date and complete and does not require advanced mathematics. However, it is tough going for those without some background in science in general and biology in particular.

R. Scott Hawley and Catherine A. Mori, *The Human Genome: A User's Guide.* San Diego: Academic Press, 1999. Hawley, a professional geneticist, and his cowriter Mori provide a clear introduction to genetics, with emphasis on those genes that determine sex and sexual development.

William K. Purves et al., *Life: The Science of Biology.* Vol. 1, *The Cell and Heredity.* Salt Lake City: Sinauer, 1998. This introduction to biology for first-year college students is clearly written and comprehensive. It is designed for those with minimal science background.

Boyce Rensberger, *Life Itself: Exploring the Realm of the Living Cell.* New York: Oxford University Press, 1996. Rensberger, science journalist, provides a good account of his subject in layman's terms. The book is useful for situating genetics within a broader discussion of cells and how they work.

Colin Tudge, *The Impact of the Gene: From Mendel's Peas to Designer Babies.* New York: Hill and Wang, 2000. Science writer Tudge discusses Mendel's work in detail and explores some of the implications of modern genetics for fields like psychology and wildlife conservation.

Articles

Tim Beardsley, "A Clone in Sheep's Clothing." *Scientific American,* March 3, 2000. Beardsley provides a brief account of the technology required to clone Dolly the sheep.

James F. Crow, *DNA Forensics: Past, Present, and Future.* Madison, WI: Promega, 2000. The article, an overview of how DNA has been used in courtrooms, includes a somewhat technical explanation of the procedures involved.

Electronic Forum on Biotechnology in Food and Agriculture, "How Appropriate Are Currently Available Biotechnologies in the Crop Sector for Food Production and Agriculture in Developing Countries." New York: Food and Agriculture Organization of the United Nations, 2000. This report analyzes the extent to which bioengineered food crops have spread throughout the world.

Virginia Cooperative Extension, "Status Report on Transgenic Organisms." Charlottesville: University of Virginia, 1997. This paper provides information on the current state of genetically engineered crops.

John Whitfield, "Obituary: Dolly the Sheep," *Nature*, February 19, 2003. Whitfield points out some of the pitfalls of animal cloning, based on the health problems and premature death of the world's first cloned mammal.

"Who We Are, How We Age, What We Eat," *Palm Beach Post*, April 12, 2002.

Internet Sources

Discovery Health Channel, "Cures," Discovery Communications, 2002. http://health.discovery.com. This overview of the applications of genetic research to medicine focuses on the feasibility of genetic cures for various diseases.

Frontline, "What Jennifer Saw," Public Broadcasting Service/ WGBH, 1998. www.pbs.org. This is a transcript of an interview with attorney Barry Scheck, one of the foremost experts on the legal aspects of genetics. He argues that DNA testing will revolutionize the criminal justice system.

Kenneth R. Bridges, "How Do People Get Sickle Cell Disease?" Harvard University, 2002. http://sickle.bwh.harvard.edu. This scholarly paper discusses the causes and consequences of sickle-cell disease, with emphasis on the mechanism of genetic inheritance.

Paul Heyman, Joanne Stark, and Ntobeko Ntusi, "ADA Deficiency," Haverford College, 1999. www.haverford.edu. The authors provide a scholarly treatment of gene therapy, using adenosine deaminase (ADA) deficiency as their primary example. Their paper is a thorough discussion of a representative genetic disease and its treatment.

Dennis O'Neil, "Mutation," Palomar College, 2002. http://anthro. palomar.edu. O'Neil discusses the process of mutation in the context of evolution. His key point is that while mutation can result in genetic disease it also plays a positive role in evolution by allowing species to adapt to changing environments.

Index

Picture Credits

About the Author

Robert Taylor is a writer and researcher with a special interest in politics, science, technology, and the history of ideas. He lives in West Palm Beach, Florida.

DATE DUE